Title 5

COUNTRIES OF THE WORLD

Sri Lanka

Gareth Stevens Publishing
A WORLD ALMANAC EDUCATION GROUP COMPANY

About the Author: Krishnan Guruswamy has worked as a writer and editor for Indian and American newspapers and news agencies for twenty-four years, during which time he also reported on Sri Lanka. He is also a photographer and specializes in photos of flowers, birds, and people.

PICTURE CREDITS

Art Directors & TRIP Photo Library: 9 (bottom), 10, 11, 14, 17, 27 (bottom), 30, 31, 35, 37, 39 (bottom), 43, 46, 57, 59, 66, 67, 87
Camera Press: 9 (top), 15 (bottom), 24, 51 (both), 61 (top), 69, 73, 80, 83
CPA Media: 1, 3 (top), 5, 7, 8, 19, 20 (bottom), 28, 40, 45 (bottom), 52, 70 (top), 89
Alain Evrard: 74, 91
Focus Team — Italy: 3 (bottom), 26, 27 (top), 33, 60
Getty Images/HultonArchive: 77 (top), 78, 79, 81, 82
GV-Press: 3 (center), 22
HBL Network Photo Agency: 6, 39 (top), 63, 64, 85
The Hutchison Library: 4, 25, 29, 34 (bottom), 38, 45 (top), 58, 61 (bottom), 65
Image Solutions: 2, 20 (top), 32, 55, 62, 77 (bottom)
John R. Jones: cover, 42, 47, 48, 49, 54, 70 (bottom), 75
Earl Kowall: 21, 23, 34 (top), 84
North Wind Picture Archives: 12, 76
Topham Picturepoint: 13, 15 (top), 15 (center), 16, 18 (both), 36, 41, 44, 50, 53, 56 (both), 68, 71, 72

Digital Scanning by Superskill Graphics Pte Ltd

Written by
KRISHNAN GURUSWAMY

Edited by
**KATHARINE BROWN
SCOTT MARSH**

Edited in the U.S. by
**MARY DYKSTRA
MONICA RAUSCH**

Designed by
LYNN CHIN

Picture research by
SUSAN JANE MANUEL

First published in North America in 2002 by
Gareth Stevens Publishing
A World Almanac Education Group Company
330 West Olive Street, Suite 100
Milwaukee, Wisconsin 53212 USA

Please visit our web site at
www.garethstevens.com
For a free color catalog describing
Gareth Stevens Publishing's list of high-quality
books and multimedia programs, call 1-800-542-2595
or fax your request to (414) 332-3567.

© **TIMES MEDIA PRIVATE LIMITED** 2002
Originated and designed by
Times Editions
An imprint of Times Media Private Limited
A member of the Times Publishing Group
Times Centre, 1 New Industrial Road
Singapore 536196
http://www.timesone.com.sg/te

Library of Congress Cataloging-in-Publication Data
Guruswamy, Krishnan.
Sri Lanka / Krishnan Guruswamy.
p. cm. — (Countries of the world)
Summary: Examines the history, geography, people, government, economy, art, and recreation of Sri Lanka.
Includes bibliographical references and index.
ISBN 0-8368-2354-0 (lib. bdg.)
1. Sri Lanka—Juvenile literature. [1. Sri Lanka.] I. Title.
II. Countries of the world (Milwaukee, Wis.)
DS489.G87 2002
954.93—dc21   2002017713

Printed in Malaysia

1 2 3 4 5 6 7 8 9 06 05 04 03 02

Contents

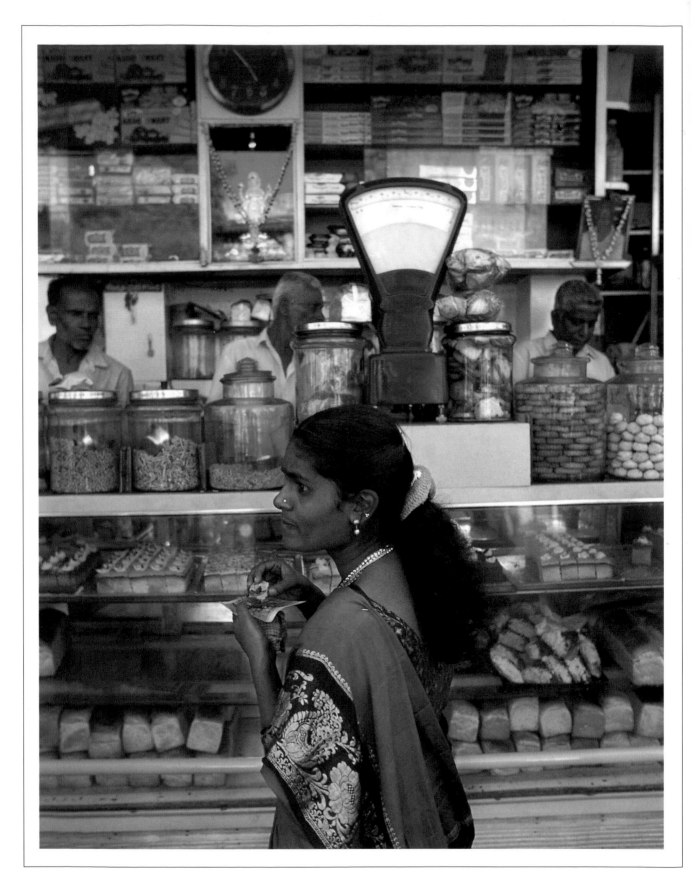

AN OVERVIEW OF SRI LANKA

Sri Lanka is known around the world for its beauty. The country is said to have been the refuge of Adam and Eve when they were sent out from the Garden of Eden. The Romans called it Taprobane, while Arab traders described it as Serendip. The Portuguese gave it the name Ceilao, which the Dutch changed to Ceylan and the British to Ceylon. The country was always known to the Sinhalese as Lanka and to the Tamils as Ilankai. In 1972, the government added the prefix *sri* (SHREE), which means "auspicious" in Sinhalese. The country has had a turbulent history since its independence from colonial rule in 1947. In recent years, Sri Lanka has experienced fighting between the military and rebels who want a homeland for the island's ethnic Tamils.

Opposite: **A woman enjoys a snack bought from a roadside shop in Sri Lanka.**

Below: **These fishermen are pulling in their nets from the ocean. Fishing provides a source of food and income for the residents of many villages near the ocean.**

THE FLAG OF THE COUNTRY

The Sri Lankan flag has two panels with a yellow border. The left panel has two vertical stripes of green and orange. The green stripe represents Sri Lanka's Muslim people. The orange stripe represents Sri Lanka's Tamil people. The right panel has a dark red background with a yellow lion holding a sword. The lion represents the Sinhalese people. Each corner of the right panel of the flag has a leaf from the sacred banyan, or bo, tree. The leaves are a symbol of Buddhism, the most popular religion in the country. These leaves were added to the flag in 1972, when the country's name was officially changed from Ceylon to Sri Lanka.

Geography

Sri Lanka is a teardrop-shaped island in the Indian Ocean, just south of India. The country has a total area of 25,332 square miles (65,610 square kilometers). Sri Lanka measures about 270 miles (434 km) north to south and 140 miles (225 km) east to west at its widest point. A chain of small islands known as the Maldives lies to the west of Sri Lanka. India is north of the country. The Palk Strait and Gulf of Mannar separate Sri Lanka and India, and a group of small islands known as Adam's Bridge lies between the two countries. There is no land south of Sri Lanka; the Indian Ocean stretches all the way to Antarctica. Singapore, Malaysia, and Indonesia lie far to the east of Sri Lanka.

Land

Sri Lanka has many different landscapes, including beaches, mountains, dense forests, arid plains, and lush hills with tea plantations. Sri Lanka has 833 miles (1,340 km) of coastline. The western, southern, and southeastern coasts of the country have

BEACHES

Sri Lanka is famous for its long stretches of beautiful beaches. The beaches attract not only local tourists but also tourists from around the world.
(A Closer Look, page 46)

Below: Galle is located along Sri Lanka's southern coast. This town is a popular tourist destination.

many lagoons and inlets, or bays. Sri Lanka's northeastern coast features several natural deep-water harbors. A mountainous area, which is surrounded by flat coastal plains, lies in the south-central part of Sri Lanka. The highest mountain is Pidurutalagala, which is 8,281 feet (2,524 meters) high. Two major plateaus in this area have many commercial tea plantations.

North of the mountains is an arid and gently rolling plain that extends to the northern tip of Sri Lanka and is known as the dry zone. Rain does not fall regularly in this area. The dry zone has many lakes, and the land in this area is usually not more than 328 feet (100 m) in height. A few rocky areas in the dry zone, however, can reach a height of 1,640 feet (500 m).

Rivers

Many rivers and streams flow through the mountainous south-central region of Sri Lanka. The longest river is the Mahaweli Ganga, which flows into the Indian Ocean south of Trincomalee. The Mahaweli Ganga starts east of Adam's Peak, a mountain that is 7,359 feet (2,243 m) high.

Above: **This man is walking along a mountain road in the town of Nuwara Eliya.**

TEA ESTATES

Tea was introduced to Sri Lanka in 1839 and has since become one of the island's major crops. The southern and central hills of Sri Lanka have many tea estates.
(A Closer Look, page 70)

7

Above: **Flowers grow easily in Sri Lanka's humid climate.**

Climate

Sri Lanka's climate is generally hot and humid since the country is near the equator. In May and June, temperatures can rise to 95° Fahrenheit (35° Celsius), with 75 percent humidity. Temperatures in the lowlands are usually around 90° F (32° C), while temperatures in the mountains are around 70° F (21° C) for most of the year. The average annual rainfall in the dry zone ranges from 47 to 75 inches (120 to 190 centimeters). In other parts of Sri Lanka, the average annual rainfall is 99 inches (251 cm).

Sri Lanka has two main seasons. The southwest monsoon, from May to August, brings rain to the southern and western parts of the country. The northeast monsoon from October to January sweeps down from the Himalayas in northern India and brings rain to the northern and eastern regions of Sri Lanka.

Plants

Sri Lanka has a great variety of beautiful plant species. Much of southwestern Sri Lanka is covered with dense tropical jungles. Thick forests grow on the mountain slopes. Timber trees, such as mahogany, are common in the wet zone of the southwest. Ebony and satinwood are common in the drier areas of Sri Lanka. Screw pines, mangroves, and many types of palm trees, such as areca, grow along the coastal areas. Other common plant species that can be found in Sri Lanka include ferns, water hyacinths, orchids, and eucalyptus trees.

Animals

Although there are many species of mammals in Sri Lanka, the elephant holds a special place in the country's culture. The species of elephant found in Sri Lanka is known as the *Elephas maximus maximus*. Other animal species include monkeys, sloth bears, porcupines, jackals, and flying foxes. Many of these animals live in wildlife sanctuaries.

More than two dozen wildlife sanctuaries are scattered across Sri Lanka. The government and many volunteer groups are working to protect Sri Lanka's wildlife. Their activities include setting up an elephant orphanage and planting trees in areas where forests have been destroyed.

Sri Lanka has more than four hundred species of birds, including bee-eaters, the Ceylon blue magpie, and the golden oriole. Sri Lanka's inland waters have more than sixty fish species, including the ornate paradise fish and red scissortail barb. About one thousand species of fish live in the coastal waters of Sri Lanka.

ELEPHANT ORPHANAGE

The Sri Lankan government has built an elephant orphanage at Pinnawela to help protect the country's elephants (*above*).
(*A Closer Look, page 54*)

Below: **Monkeys play among the ruins of an ancient building in Anuradhapura.**

History

The original inhabitants of Sri Lanka were the Wanniyala-Aettos, or *Veddahs* (VED-duhs). Most historians believe that in the fifth or sixth century B.C., people from northern India settled on the island and came to be known as the Sinhalese. The Sinhalese kingdom developed in the northern plains, and its capital was Anuradhapura. Buddhism was introduced to Sri Lanka in the third century B.C., when the Anuradhapura king and his followers became Buddhists. Anuradhapura remained the kingdom's capital until the tenth century A.D. In the eleventh century A.D., the Sinhalese capital was shifted southeast to Polonnaruwa where it remained for two hundred years. Up until the twelfth century A.D., Tamils from southern India invaded and occupied Anuradhapura several times. The Tamils eventually established their kingdom in northern Sri Lanka. In the twelfth and thirteenth centuries, Sinhalese princes briefly gained power over the Tamil kingdom. The island also was attacked by Chinese, Malayan, and southern Indian forces until the first European powers arrived in 1505.

ANURADHAPURA & POLONNARUWA

The ruins of the ancient capital cities of Anuradhapura and Polonnaruwa still stand today.
(*A Closer Look, page 44*)

Below: **Tourists visit the remains of an ancient palace in Polonnaruwa.**

Colonial Period

Spices were valuable luxury goods in Europe during the sixteenth century, and the Portuguese, Dutch, French, and British sailed to the East in search of these goods. The Portuguese were the first European power to reach Sri Lanka, which, at that time was made up of three main kingdoms — two Sinhalese kingdoms in Kandy and Kotte (now Sri Jayewardenepura Kotte) and a Tamil kingdom in Jaffna. In 1505, a Portuguese fleet was sailing from India in search of spice ships to attack when it was was caught in a storm that brought it to Sri Lanka. The Portuguese were given permission to build a fort and were granted trade concessions in 1518. They formed alliances with the local rulers. Whenever they had the chance, the Portuguese appointed kings who would be loyal to them. Political scheming and military conquests enabled the Portuguese to gain control of most of Sri Lanka by 1619. The only area the Portuguese did not capture was the kingdom of Kandy in the central mountains of Sri Lanka. Kandyan rulers asked the Dutch to help them drive the Portuguese out of Sri Lanka, and the Dutch launched their first attacks in 1638.

Above: **Kandy was not captured by Portuguese invaders in the sixteenth century. The rulers of Kandy later formed an alliance with the Dutch to drive the Portuguese out of Sri Lanka.**

Left: **These factory workers are sorting and grading dried tea leaves on a plantation in Sri Lanka at the beginning of the twentieth century.**

Dutch Rule

The local population found the Portuguese to be oppressive rulers, and many locals helped the Dutch fight the Portuguese. The Dutch and their Sri Lankan allies fought the Portuguese for about twenty years. Finally, the Dutch gained control of most of the island in 1658, although the kingdom of Kandy remained independent. The Dutch concentrated on the spice trade and did not interfere much in the lives of the people. Dutch forces governed Sri Lanka until 1796, when the Dutch surrendered to invading British forces.

British Rule

Although the Dutch formally ceded the island to Great Britain in 1802, the kingdom of Kandy remained independent. In 1815, however, the British succeeded in gaining control of Kandy. The British promoted the establishment of coffee, tea, and coconut plantations; built railroads to transport goods; and taught English in schools and colleges. In 1817, 1843, and 1848, Sri Lankan forces mounted unsuccessful rebellions against the British. Sri Lankans struggled for decades to gain independence from the British. Finally in 1931, Britain gave Sri Lanka limited control over its national affairs. During World War II, Sri Lanka became a base for British forces in Southeast Asia.

Independence at Last

At the end of World War II, the Sri Lankan people increased pressure on the British for independence. They were partly encouraged by the independence movement in neighboring India. In 1947, the British granted Sri Lanka independence.

The first post-colonial government was led by Prime Minister Don Stephen Senanayake. An ancient Sinhalese flag was adopted as the flag of the new state. When Senanayake died in 1952, his son, Dudley Senanayake, succeeded him as prime minister.

In 1956, Solomon West Ridgeway Dias Bandaranaike came to power. He campaigned against the English language, Western clothes, and Christianity, all of which were symbols of European culture. After coming to power, Bandaranaike adopted policies that favored the country's Sinhalese people. These policies created much tension between the country's Sinhalese and Tamil populations. The simmering tensions would lead to a civil war several decades later.

WOMEN LEADERS

Sirimavo Ratwatte Dias Bandaranaike (1916–2000) was the world's first woman prime minister. Her daughter, Chandrika Bandaranaike Kumaratunga (1945–), was elected president of Sri Lanka in 1994.
(A Closer Look, page 72)

Below: **S.W.R.D. Bandaranaike (***second from right***), Sri Lanka's prime minister from 1956 to 1959, shares a snack with his children.**

Troubled Times

Bandaranaike was assassinated in 1959, and his wife, Sirimavo Bandaranaike, was elected prime minister the following year. She made Sinhala the sole official language of the country in 1960, a move that triggered demonstrations among the country's Tamil people. After losing the 1965 elections to Dudley Senanayake, Bandaranaike returned to power in 1970 and continued implementing policies that discriminated against Tamils. In the 1970s, several anti-government guerrilla groups were formed. By 1983, a guerrilla group known as the Liberation Tigers of Tamil Eelam (LTTE) emerged as Sri Lanka's main Tamil guerrilla group.

In 1983, LTTE guerrillas killed thirteen army soldiers. This event sparked an anti-Tamil riot, and a civil war has engulfed the island ever since. In 1994, Chandrika Bandaranaike Kumaratunga was elected president. After her initial peace talks with the LTTE failed, war broke out again. In 2001, a new prime minister, Ranil Wickremesinghe, was elected in parliamentary elections. He has promised to resume peace talks with the LTTE. Kumaratunga will serve as president until the next presidential elections in 2005.

TAMIL TIGERS

The Liberation Tigers of Tamil Eelam, or Tamil Tigers, are fighting for an independent Tamil homeland in Sri Lanka.
(*A Closer Look*, page 68)

CIVIL WAR

Sri Lankan government forces (*below*) and Tamil separatists have been fighting each other in a civil war since 1983.
(*A Closer Look*, page 50)

Solomon West Ridgeway Dias Bandaranaike (1899–1959)

S.W.R.D. Bandaranaike studied law at Oxford University in Britain. He practiced law in Sri Lanka, and then entered politics and became a federal lawmaker in 1947. He encouraged the Sinhala language and arts and championed the rights of the poor. He founded the Sri Lanka Freedom Party (SLFP) and was elected prime minister in 1956. Bandaranaike believed that political freedom should be used to achieve freedom from hunger, poverty, ignorance, and disease. His decisions to make Sinhala the official language and give Buddhism a more important place in the country, however, angered the country's minorities and laid the foundation for conflict. He was assassinated by a Sinhala monk in 1959.

S.W.R.D.
Bandaranaike

Sirimavo Ratwatte Dias Bandaranaike (1916–2000)

Bandaranaike entered politics in 1960 after her husband, Prime Minister S.W.R.D. Bandaranaike, was killed. Her government took over many American and British companies and changed the name of the country from Ceylon to Sri Lanka. She ordered all government work to be carried out in Sinhala and changed university admission policies to benefit the Sinhalese, which angered the country's ethnic Tamils. Bandaranaike lost Sri Lanka's 1965 elections but was re-elected prime minister in 1970. She lost the 1977 elections and spent the next seventeen years as an opposition politician before becoming prime minister again in 1994.

Sirimavo Ratwatte
Dias Bandaranaike

Velupillai Prabhakaran (1954–)

Prabhakaran is the leader of the Liberation Tigers of Tamil Eelam, often referred to as the Tigers or Tamil Tigers. This guerrilla group wants to create a Tamil homeland called *Eelam* (EE-lahm), meaning "precious land," in northern and eastern Sri Lanka. His group has been blamed for several bombings and assassinations. Prabhakaran operates from a secret base in the jungles of northeast Sri Lanka. He studied guerrilla warfare tactics and trained himself to withstand torture.

Velupillai
Prabhakaran

Government and the Economy

Sri Lanka is a democracy, with a president and national parliament elected by the people. Anyone aged eighteen and older has the right to vote. The president is both the chief of state and head of government. The office of the president was established through changes to the country's constitution in 1978. The prime minister had previously headed government. The national parliament has only one house with 225 seats, and parliament members serve six-year terms.

The country is divided into nine provinces. The president appoints a governor for each province, and voters elect provincial councils, which have five-year terms. The leader of the political party with the most seats on a council becomes the chief minister of the province. The councils have powers over education, health, social services, agriculture, and local taxation. They share many of these powers with the federal government.

Below: **Sri Lanka's old parliament building in Colombo now houses the offices of the country's Presidential Secretariat (president's administrative staff).**

Left: Sri Lanka's first president was William Gopallawa (1897–1981). He held the post from 1972 to 1978. Under his successor, Junius Jayewardene, the powers of the presidency were strengthened.

Judiciary

The Sri Lankan judicial system consists of the Supreme Court, the Court of Appeal, the High Court, and many lower courts, such as the primary and district courts. The Supreme Court has eleven justices including the chief justice. The Supreme Court justices and the judges of the Court of Appeal and High Court are appointed by Sri Lanka's president. Judges from the lower courts are appointed by the Judicial Service Commission, which is made up of the chief justice and two judges of the Supreme Court.

Political Parties

Sri Lanka has more than twenty recognized political parties. Some of the main groups are the People's Alliance, which includes the Sri Lanka Freedom Party; United National Party; People's Liberation Front; Sri Lanka Muslim Congress; and Tamil United Liberation Front. The People's Alliance, which is an alliance of several parties, first won the general elections in 1994. In the next election, in 2000, the People's Alliance was the single largest group in parliament. In 2001 parliamentary elections, the United National Party won the majority, with about 45 percent of the vote.

Left: About 15 percent of the land in Sri Lanka is under cultivation. Agriculture contributes a large amount of money to the country's export earnings.

Economy

From independence in 1948 until 1977, successive governments in Sri Lanka followed policies that discouraged private businesses. The government ran schools, hospitals, and bus and train services, as well as businesses. Although services were either free or subsidized, the government-run agencies were often inefficient and corrupt. In 1977, the country's government began encouraging private businesses and export-oriented trade. A small number of American and European companies opened up in Sri Lanka, attracted by the low wages they would have to pay.

Sri Lanka's main exports are garments, tea, gems, and spices. The foreign currency earned through exports is used to buy gasoline, arms and ammunition, and other goods. Sri Lankans who work overseas are another major source of foreign currency, as they send home money every year.

The Sri Lankan civil war has placed a great strain on the country's economy. Frequent gun battles and bomb blasts in civilian areas have scared away tourists, who provide jobs to thousands of people. The national labor force of about seven million is mostly employed in agriculture and the service industry.

GEMS

Precious stones (*above*), such as diamonds, are one of Sri Lanka's main exports.
(*A Closer Look*, page 56)

COLOMBO

Colombo is the business center of Sri Lanka. It is also the country's largest city.
(*A Closer Look*, page 52)

Transportation

Sri Lanka has a network of 6,662 miles (10,721 km) of paved roads. Buses connect most parts of the country and are the most popular form of transportation even though many buses are noisy and outdated. Gasoline is imported and expensive. Few people can afford a car or a motorcycle. Trains link important Sri Lankan cities on a network that is 909 miles (1,463 km) long. The service is subsidized by the government.

Employment

Sri Lanka's unemployment rate is close to 9 percent, and 22 percent of the population lives below the poverty line. The country has a number of industries, including agriculture, clothing, cement, petroleum refining, textiles, tobacco, and service industries. Many Sri Lankans are employed overseas as factory workers and domestic help, where they earn wages several times higher than they would get back home. Government jobs are in great demand because these guarantee employment and pension benefits.

Below: **Passengers wait to board a train at a Colombo train station.**

People and Lifestyle

Ethnic Groups

The indigenous people of Sri Lanka are the Wanniyala-Aettos, known in Sinhalese as the Veddahs. They are forest dwellers who are believed to have lived in the country for thousands of years. About 2,500 Veddahs still live deep in the southeastern forests. These Veddahs continue to follow their traditional way of life. They hunt wild animals for food and gather honey and other forest products.

Sri Lanka has four main ethnic groups apart from the Veddahs: Sinhalese; Tamils; Moors, or Muslims; and Burghers. No physical traits distinguish each of these four groups. The Sinhalese account for 74 percent of the population. They came to Sri Lanka around the fifth century B.C. from northern India and later became Buddhists.

Beginning around the third century A.D., Tamils from southern India invaded the country and eventually established a kingdom in northern Sri Lanka. The Tamils are mostly Hindu although a small number are Christians. The language, religion, and cultural practices of the Tamils are completely different from those of the Sinhalese.

SARIS AND REDDE-HATTES

Many Sri Lankan women wear traditional clothes known as saris (*above*). (*A Closer Look, page 64*)

Below: **These women enjoy a stroll along a street in Colombo.**

Tamils form about 18 percent of the population and consist of two groups: Sri Lankan Tamils and Indian Tamils. Tamils whose ancestors settled in the country more than one thousand years ago are known as Sri Lankan, or Ceylon, Tamils. The ancestors of the other group, the Indian Tamils, were brought from southern India by the British in the nineteenth century to work on plantations in the hills of central Sri Lanka.

Moors constitute 7 percent of the population. They speak Tamil and are Muslims, or followers of Islam. Moors are believed to be descendants of Arab and Muslim Indian spice traders.

A fourth ethnic group is the Burghers, who form less than 1 percent of the population. They are descendants of Portuguese and Dutch invaders. A handful of descendants of Chinese, other Europeans, and Malays also are scattered all over the country.

The division between the rich and the poor is very wide in Sri Lanka. Children of the wealthy often go to private schools, where they are taught English, and later study at universities abroad. Less wealthy Sri Lankans go to state universities, where the language of instruction is mostly Sinhala.

Above: **It is common to see several generations of family members living under one roof in Sri Lanka, especially in rural areas.**

Family Life

Many Sri Lankans live in extended families in which people from several generations live in the same house. Increasing Westernization and urbanization, however, are beginning to create more nuclear families, with just parents and their children. Divorce is rare. Sri Lanka has a strong family planning program, and the population growth rate is low, at about 1 percent. Parents often decide what their children should study in school and what careers they should pursue. Age is respected in Sri Lanka, and children and young adults tend to cater to their elders.

Marriages are decided by parents, mostly based on class and the astrological charts of the bride and groom. Dating and choosing one's partner are rare, as Sri Lankan culture does not encourage public courtship. Even holding hands in public is discouraged. Increased Westernization is changing these customs, however, and it is now more common to see young men and women courting in public in the country's cities and large towns.

From childhood, girls are brought up to believe that caring for their future husbands is one of their most important tasks in life. Boys are taught that they must provide not only for their

Above: **Sri Lankan children are expected to obey their parents, even when they become adults.**

wives and children but also for their parents during old age. By the time children are in their early twenties, their parents start to look for suitable marriage partners. When they decide that their daughter or son should marry — usually when he or she gets a job — the parents advertise in newspapers, tell their friends, or contact a commercial marriage broker.

Arranged Marriages

When a marriage is being arranged, a family astrologer first compares the horoscopes of the man and woman. If the horoscopes are compatible, the families of the man and woman meet formally, usually in the woman's home. The couple is allowed to chat for a short while in another room. If both of them agree to be married and their parents approve, the families begin to discuss the terms. The parents of the bride are expected to pay a hefty dowry, in cash or land. The dowry is higher if the man is wealthy and educated. Once the wedding is over, the couple is often pressured by relatives to have a baby. Sons are usually preferred over daughters as male children inherit the family property and surname.

FUNERAL PYRES

Buddhist and Hindu traditions advocate respect for elders. Sons, for example, are required to light the funeral pyres of their parents.

Below: This Sri Lankan couple is wearing traditional clothes for their wedding ceremony. Many marriages in Sri Lanka are arranged by family members.

23

Education

Sri Lanka has a literacy rate of 90 percent. Sri Lanka's cities and villages have many elementary schools, although some classes are cramped with forty-five to fifty-five students. Sri Lanka has about four million students and 200,000 teachers.

All education — from preschool to university — is free. Sri Lankan children between the ages of five and fourteen must attend school. Most children attend five years of elementary school, four years of middle school, two years of high school, and two years of pre-university courses. They study English and either Sinhala or Tamil as well as subjects such as mathematics, life sciences, and social studies. These subjects are usually taught in Sinhala or Tamil. After eleven years of school, students can take the test for the General Certificate of Education, or O level. To be awarded a full certificate they must pass six subjects, including languages.

In the pre-university program, which covers three subjects, students can specialize in either the sciences or humanities. At the end of the program students take a written examination, known

Below: **These children in Sri Lanka are attending a class taught by a Buddhist monk.**

as the General Certificate of Education, or A level. Students who want to enter a university must score at least 140 points and pass another test called a Common General Test.

Above: **These Sri Lankan students are enjoying a break between classes. The literacy rate of Sri Lankan women is about 83 percent.**

After coming home from school, many children have private tutoring classes, usually in mathematics and science. Private tutoring is expensive, and parents save to pay for it. Most children are pressured by their parents to get high grades in school so they can enter Sri Lanka's top universities.

The most popular university programs are medicine, law, engineering and computer science. Competition to enter these faculties is fierce. Most students try to earn a university degree. Without a degree, their opportunities are generally limited to unskilled or manual labor.

Students who drop out of school usually try to learn a trade, such as carpentry, or work with a skilled craftsperson. The country's few trade schools, however, cannot meet the country's demand for skilled technicians and craftspersons.

Universities in Sri Lanka offer degrees in a variety of subjects. Some wealthy parents try to send their children to India, Canada, England, Australia, or the United States for higher education.

Above: These
Sri Lankan boys
are attending
religious classes in
a Buddhist temple.

Religion

Sri Lanka has four main religions: Buddhism, Hinduism,
Christianity, and Islam. Religious instruction is given in schools,
and the school day usually begins with prayer. Many schools
incorporate prayers from Sri Lanka's four main religions.

Seventy percent of Sri Lanka's population follow Buddhism.
This religion is not centered around the worship of a god. Instead,
Buddhism is based on a system of beliefs that emphasizes love,
compassion, and gentleness.

Buddhism was founded when an Indian prince named
Siddhartha Gautama left his kingdom to meditate under a banyan
tree. After meditating, he became enlightened; he discovered why
life is filled with sufferings. He was then known as the Buddha.
Buddha preached that all life is suffering, and people suffer
because they have desires. People can end their suffering by
getting rid of their desires in eight ways: right speech, right
thought, right understanding, right action, right livelihood,
right attentiveness, right concentration, and right effort.

About 15 percent of Sri Lankans practice Hinduism. This faith
was brought to the island by the Tamils of southern India, who

BUDDHIST DAGOBAS

Buddhist *dagobas*
(DAH-go-bahs) have
been built in many
parts of Sri Lanka.
(A Closer Look, page 48)

often invaded the island. The main belief of Hinduism is in *Brahman* (BRAH-mahn), a supreme being. There is only one Brahman, but Hindus have hundreds of gods and goddesses who are all forms of Brahman. The most important Hindu gods are Brahma, the god of creation; Vishnu, the god of preservation; and Shiva, the god of destruction.

About 8 percent of Sri Lanka's population is Christian. Christianity came to Sri Lanka in the sixteenth century with Portuguese colonizers who converted the locals to Roman Catholicism. The Dutch brought Protestantism in the seventeenth century, and the British introduced other Christian denominations over one hundred years later.

Seven percent of Sri Lankans follow Islam, which was founded in the seventh century by the Prophet Mohammed. Muslims believe in surrendering themselves to their God, called Allah. In Islam, God has no equal or partner, and everything in the world is created by God. Muslims believe God spoke to people through messengers such as the Prophet Mohammed. After Mohammed's death, followers of Islam split into two groups: Sunnis and Shias, or Shiites. Arab and Indian traders brought Islam to Sri Lanka. Most of the Muslims on the island are Sunnis. According to their Islamic beliefs, Muslims should pray five times a day, donate money to charity, and fast for one month each year.

Above: A relatively small number of Sri Lankans are Muslims. This boy is wearing a *ketayap* (kur-TAH-yahp), a type of headdress worn by Muslim men and boys.

KARMA AND DHARMA

Hindus believe in rebirth and that the quality of life depends on a person's karma and dharma. Karma refers to how a person's conduct or action in previous lives affects his or her present life. Dharma refers to the right or proper way a person should behave.

Left: This biblical scene is on display outside a Catholic church in the city of Negombo.

Language and Literature

Language

Sri Lanka has two national languages: Sinhala, or Sinhalese, and Tamil. About 74 percent of Sri Lanka's population speaks Sinhala, which can trace its origins to an ancient language called Sanskrit. Many Sinhalese words are similar to those found in the languages of Europe, Iran, and northern India. Sinhala was also influenced by the Tamil, Portuguese, Dutch, and English languages.

Tamil is spoken by about three to four million Sri Lankans. Tamil is one of the world's oldest languages and was spoken in southern India before Indo-European languages were introduced.

Only a small percentage of Sri Lankans speak English, although many Sri Lankans understand the language. Sri Lanka has its own unique English phrases. For example, "short eats" are snacks, a "batchmate" is a classmate, and a "purse" is a wallet.

SRI LANKAN GREETINGS

Ayubovan (AH-yooh-boh-vahn) and *Vanakkam* (vah-nah-KAHM) are Sinhala and Tamil greetings, respectively, that roughly mean welcome. You greet a Sri Lankan by holding your palms pressed together in front of your chest and bowing slightly.

Below: These signs in Colombo are written in Sinhala.

Many Sinhala and Tamil words are also part of the English language. For example, the English word "cash" is from a Tamil word, *kaasu* (KAH-sooh), which means "ready money."

Above: The literacy rate among Sri Lanka's population is high.

Literature

Sinhala and Tamil literature date back more than two thousand years. Ancient Tamil and Sinhalese works were written on palm leaves. One of the earliest known written works in Sri Lanka is the *Mahavamsa*, which records the history of the island. The Tamils who invaded Sri Lanka brought with them their rich literature.

Sinhala prose written between the tenth and thirteenth centuries told the life story of the Buddha and of kings. From the fifteenth to the nineteenth centuries, Sinhalese writers used poetry to express their views. From the late nineteenth century, Sinhalese and Tamil writers began to write non-religious stories, as well as textbooks on medicine and science. In the 1950s, prose and poetry dealt mainly with problems of independence. Earlier stories were often about colonial rule, but a new generation of Sri Lankan-born writers, who live outside the country, has risen to prominence. Little Sri Lankan writing is in English.

SRI LANKAN AUTHORS
Some Sri Lankan authors, such as Ambalavaner Sivanandan, have become world famous. Sivanandan won the Commonwealth Writers Prize in 1998 in the Asia-Oceania region for *When Memory Dies*, an account of three generations of a Sri Lankan family. Other well-known writers include Shyam Selvadurai, Romesh Gunesekera, and Michael Ondaatje.

Arts

Music

Pop and film music, which are also called light music in Sri Lanka, are popular throughout the country, and films usually feature five or six songs. Light music has drawn from the rich tradition of street theater and southern Indian classical music. Ananda Samarakone is regarded as a pioneer of Sinhala light music, and he also composed Sri Lanka's national anthem. Pandit W. D. Amaradeva is one of the country's leading musicians and vocalists. He won the Magsaysay Award for Journalism, Literature, and Creative Communication Arts in 2001.

The Sinhala *baila* (BY-lah) is an energetic and pulsating music, similar to Caribbean calypso, but with throbbing drums. Baila songs are sung in many versions as they allow for on-the-spot improvisations, which can be funny and entertaining. Baila is often played at community dances.

The British introduced Western classical music to Sri Lanka, and some music and stage groups perform operas. Sri Lankans also enjoy music from all over the world.

SUNIL SANTHA

Sunil Santha (1915–1981), a popular Sri Lankan singer and musician, helped define modern Sri Lankan music. While many of his fellow musicians put Sinhalese lyrics to Indian tunes, Santha composed many beautiful songs and melodies himself.

Below: A band puts on a lively performance beside a temple.

Left: Watching movies is a popular activity in Sri Lanka. The country has many cinemas showing local and foreign films.

Movies

Sri Lankans enjoy watching movies. The country has many movie theaters, and tickets are relatively inexpensive. Early movies were often local versions of foreign films. The first movie in Sinhalese, *Broken Promise*, was made in 1947.

In the 1950s, after independence and the emergence of nationalism, Sri Lankan directors began to focus on local themes. In 1970, the government took over the film industry and set up a distribution company. Directors began to experiment with issues facing society, such as Sri Lanka's ethnic tensions. The film industry declined in the 1990s because of restrictive distribution practices. In January 2000, the government relinquished its control of the film industry.

Today, the most popular director is Lester James Peiris, who won the Lifetime Achievement Award at the International Film Festival in India in 2000. Peiris and his wife, Sumitra, have produced dozens of award-winning films. Other popular directors are Vasantha Obeysekera and H. D. Premaratne.

Dance

Dance is a major art form in Sinhalese and Tamil traditional life. The Kandyan dance, a dance form that flourished during the time of the Kandyan kings, is considered the national dance of Sri Lanka. Male dancers wear a wide skirt and silver and ivory necklaces on their bare chests. Female dancers wear a skirt and short blouse with silver embroidery. Dancers leap and twirl in the air, accompanied by drummers playing complex rhythms.

Other forms of dance include the devil dance and *kolam* (KOH-lahm) dance. The devil dance is usually performed to exorcise evil spirits. The devil dance is seldom seen now, as it is becoming increasingly expensive to perform. Kolam dance performances are held once a year over a period of seven to ten nights. A kolam dance has many different characters who wear masks. Many of these masks look like monsters and represent demons in kolam dances.

Above: **The complex patterns of batik prints require plenty of skill and patience.**

Handicrafts

Wooden masks and mats of plant fiber are among the important handicrafts of Sri Lanka. Earthen pots are still sold on the roadsides, and a large number of people still use them for cooking food. Cloth dyers specialize in batik. In this special art form, the dyers spend hours drawing designs on cloth with melted wax before dyeing the patterns in many colors.

MASKS

Masks are an important part of Sri Lankan culture and are used in many types of traditional dances and plays.
(*A Closer Look*, page 60)

Architecture

Sri Lankan Buddhist architecture is best seen in the brick dagobas, or Buddhist shrines, that are found in the northern parts of the country. Most dagobas are shaped like a dome or a bell and are white. Dagobas are made from bricks and then covered by a layer of plaster.

Hindu temples, or *kovils* (KOH-vills), are often dedicated to the worship of Shiva, the god of destruction. Hindu temples contain a prayer hall and shrine room. A covered path enables worshipers to walk around the prayer hall and shrine room. Some temples have tall, brightly colored *gopurams* (go-POOH-rahms), or gateways.

Many buildings in Sri Lanka have traces of European architecture from the years when Sri Lanka was ruled first by the Portuguese, then by the Dutch, and finally by the British. This influence can be seen in buildings such as forts and churches.

HINDU TEMPLES

Many Hindu temples contain elaborate sculptures. Sri Lankans are still working to restore Hindu temples destroyed by the Portuguese over two hundred years ago.
(*A Closer Look*, page 58)

Opposite: **A traditional dance troupe performs at a hotel in Sri Lanka.**

Leisure and Festivals

Children

School children are good at inventing games that do not require expensive equipment and that they can play in the few minutes they have between classes. Most children like to play hide-and-seek, chase each other in a park or apartment building, or hurl rocks at fruit on trees or at a target. Even simple activities, such as rolling a bicycle tire down a road, are a source of enjoyment and entertainment for children.

Traditional Activities

Traditional games are played mostly during the New Year celebrations in April and at national festivals. In one game, participants try to climb up a greased pole to get a flag placed at the top. Another popular game is *kotta pora* (koh-TAH POH-rah), or pillow fighting. Competitors sit on a pole and try to knock each other off using pillows.

Storytelling has long been popular in Sri Lanka, especially in rural areas. Grandparents traditionally gathered the children around them at dusk to tell them folktales.

Above: **Cycling is a popular pastime in Sri Lanka.**

Left: **Batik printing is a traditional activity that has been passed down from one generation to the next in Sri Lanka.**

Indoor Activities

Indoor games, such as chess, checkers, and regional variations of Monopoly, are popular in cities. One Sri Lankan indoor game is known as *olinda kaliya* (oh-LIN-dah KAH-lee-yah). The game is usually played on a wooden board that has two rows of small hollowed-out sections, or pits. Each end of the board has one large pit. Players place red seeds around the board and try to capture all their opponent's seeds. The first player to place all of his or her seeds on his or her end of the board wins the game.

Outdoor Fun

Popular outdoor activities include swimming and fishing, which is not surprising since Sri Lanka has many beaches, rivers, and lakes. Wealthy Sri Lankans play games such as tennis and squash or exercise in health centers. Bicycle riding is a popular activity with both the young and old. Sri Lankans who prefer less strenuous exercise enjoy going for walks along the country's beautiful beaches or in the countryside while chatting with their friends and family.

Sports

Sri Lanka has much to offer sports enthusiasts, and many sports, including golf, cycling, cricket, and various types of water sports, are played in Sri Lanka.

Sri Lanka currently has three golf courses, with more being planned. Sri Lanka's largest golf tournament is sponsored by Sri Lankan Airlines, the country's national airline. The tournament, known as the Sri Lankan Airlines Golf Classic, is usually held every October. The event attracts dozens of foreign players as well as many local players each year.

Many of Sri Lanka's top hotels have tennis courts that are also open to players who are not hotel guests. Tennis clubs are more exclusive; the courts are only open to members. Several tennis clubs are located in Colombo and other major cities.

Bicycle riding is a popular sport in Sri Lanka. Bicycles can be rented in most Sri Lankan cities, and cycling is one of the best ways to see Sri Lanka's beautiful countryside. Many Sri Lankan roads are in poor condition, however, and bicycles can be damaged by excessive wear and tear.

Above: **Two members of Sri Lanka's national cricket team congratulate each other on a play during a match against England in 1996. Sri Lanka won the 1996 Cricket World Cup.**

Cricket has been the most popular sport in Sri Lanka since the sport was brought to the island by British colonialists. The sport became even more popular after Sri Lanka's triumph in the 1996 Cricket World Cup tournament. Members of Sri Lanka's national team are regarded as heroes, and many schoolboys aspire to represent their country in international competitions. Sri Lanka's cricket season runs from September to April each year, and there are many stadiums in Sri Lanka where spectators can go to cheer for their favorite local teams.

Water Sports

Sri Lanka has many beautiful beaches with clear, unpolluted water, and water sports, including diving and snorkeling, are favorites with locals and tourists.

Good diving spots can be found around Sri Lanka, especially near Galle and Colombo. Divers and snorkelers can see interesting underwater scenery, including marine life, coral reefs, and even several shipwrecks that divers can explore. Sri Lanka's diving seasons are relatively short, however, because diving during monsoons can be dangerous.

SANATH TERAN JAYASURIYA

Sanath Teran Jayasuriya is one of Sri Lanka's most popular cricket players. He was named the most valuable player of Sri Lanka's 1996 series.

Below: Besides cricket, Sri Lankans enjoy playing soccer and basketball. These basketball teams are playing in a local competition.

Festivals

Sri Lankans enjoy nearly thirty public holidays a year celebrating the country's Buddhist, Hindu, Muslim, and Christian festivals. The Sri Lankan New Year falls on April 14 and coincides with the end of the harvest season. This holiday also marks the beginning of the southwest monsoon. Early in the morning on this holiday, a large drum is beaten to herald the new year. Adults and children rub their bodies with oil before bathing. At an auspicious time decided by priests and announced on television, the first fire of the new year is lighted in the hearth, and the mother or an elder woman of the house boils milk over it to make milk rice. The family then wears new clothes and eats the first meal together. Children set off firecrackers to welcome the new year. Later, families visit their neighbors and relatives and exchange fruit baskets and gifts.

Vesak is a major Buddhist holiday that is celebrated in May. This festival celebrates the birth, enlightenment, and death of Buddha. Large billboards that show scenes from the Buddha's life are set up on street corners and in villages. Paper lanterns are hung from trees and buildings, and oil lamps are lit at night.

PERAHERA

Perahera (peh-RAH-HEH-rah) **is a grand procession held in the city of Kandy. The procession is made in honor of Kandy's holy relic, the Sacred Tooth of Buddha.**
(A Closer Look, page 62)

Below: **A Hindu priest leads a woman devotee in a chant during a temple festival.**

Sri Lanka's major Hindu holiday is Deepavali, which occurs in late October or early November. Deepavali marks the triumph of good over evil. *Thai Pongal* (THIGH POHNG-gahl) is a Hindu harvest festival celebrated in January. The other major Hindu festival is *Thaipusam* (THIGH-poo-sum). Those who participate in this festival must pray and fast for about one month. Some participants pierce their tongues, cheeks, or backs with small skewers as symbols of penance. During the festival, some participants run barefoot over a bed of red-hot coals — and come away with no burns.

Above and *below:* **The colorful Perahera in Kandy attracts thousands of Buddhists from all over Sri Lanka.**

Sri Lanka's Muslims observe Ramadan in December or January. During this time, healthy adults fast throughout the day and eat only between dusk and dawn. The last day of the fast is celebrated as *Id-ul-Fitr* (eed-OOL-FIT-ruh). The other major Islamic holiday is *Milad-un-Nabi* (MEE-LAHD-un-nah-bee), which marks the birthday of the Prophet Mohammed.

Christmas and Good Friday are the major Christian holidays in Sri Lanka. Christmas celebrates the birth of Jesus Christ, and Good Friday commemorates Christ's death on the cross.

Food

Many Sri Lankan dishes consist of rice, various vegetables, and seafood. Toast and omelettes, served with tea, are popular breakfast dishes among many Sri Lankans. For breakfast in traditional homes, especially in rural areas, women light a wooden stove to cook rice-based dishes, such as *hoppers* (hop-PERS), string hoppers, and *pittu* (pit-TOOH). To make hoppers, women pour a rice mixture into small earthen bowls. Then they cover the bowls and heat them slowly. Sometimes they break an egg in the middle of the hoppers while they are being cooked. Hoppers sometimes are eaten with a vegetable stew spiced with cinnamon. String hoppers are steamed circles of rice noodles that are eaten with spiced gravy. Pittu is a mixture of rice flour and grated coconut steamed in a bamboo tube. *Sambal* (SAHM-bahl), a chutney of grated coconut, chili peppers, and spices, is a popular side dish.

A typical lunch or dinner consists of rice and curry. Rice is dished onto a plate and is eaten with spicy vegetables, meat, fish,

COCONUTS

The juice, or milk, from coconuts is a good thirst quencher, especially in summer. Coconut vendors in Sri Lanka sit on piles of coconuts on roadsides. When a customer buys a coconut, the vendor uses a machete to lop off the top of the coconut. After the juice is gone, the soft white pulp of the coconut can be eaten as a snack.

Below: Sri Lankan dishes are often spicy.

40

Above: **A stall owner sells fried snacks in a Sri Lankan village.**

lentils, and sambal. Sri Lankan curries are hot; fresh or dried chili peppers are ground with spices and coconut milk to add flavor. Sri Lankans eat with their right hands, and they say the food is tastier when eaten with the fingers. Cutlery is used in some urban homes or provided for foreign guests.

Snacks include meat or vegetable rolls and patties. One popular snack is *vadai* (VAH-day), a deep-fried patty of lentils and flour. *Rotty* (ROH-tea), another snack, is like a soft tortilla wrapped around a mixture of meat and vegetables or just onions and chili peppers. Desserts include *wattalappam* (WAH-TAHL-ah-pum), an egg pudding that has a caramel-like flavor; *aluva* (AH-loo-ah), a rice-flour fudge; and yogurt with palm syrup.

A wide variety of tropical fruits grows in Sri Lanka. Rambutan is a native walnut-sized fruit covered with red hairs that contains a sweet, fleshy pulp. Pineapples are abundant throughout Sri Lanka, and roadside vendors often sell them in slices. Mangoes, also grown in the country, are soft, orange-colored pulpy fruits that can be mildly sweet or very sweet, depending on their origin.

Tea is the most popular non-alcoholic drink throughout the country. Sri Lanka is one of the world's major tea producers.

SPICES

Spices are an important ingredient in any Sri Lankan recipe. Sri Lankan spices are also exported throughout the world.

(A Closer Look, page 66)

A CLOSER LOOK AT SRI LANKA

Sri Lanka is renowned for its vibrant history, culture, and people. The magnificent cities, structures, and irrigation systems built by ancient Sri Lankan rulers hundreds of years ago are still considered architectural marvels today. Buddhist kings built enormous shrines in honor of the Buddha, while Hindu rulers imitated temple architecture from neighboring India. Stunning Muslim mosques and Christian churches stand in this diverse and beautiful country. Sri Lanka's Portuguese, Dutch, and British colonial rulers have also left their marks on the country's culture, language, and architecture.

Below: **These dancers dressed in traditional clothes are taking part in a street parade in Colombo.**

Today, Sri Lanka is known for stunning beaches, a wide variety of gems, aromatic spices, and lush tea estates. Elephants are a major part of Sri Lankan life, and they are used in religious ceremonies by Buddhists and Hindus. Traditional practices, such as mask-carving and performing street plays, are still followed in Sri Lanka. Colorful festivals honor the country's four main religions. Unfortunately, this country, which has enchanted travelers for centuries, is in the midst of a violent civil war. For more than a decade, ethnic fighting has rocked the country and continues to threaten its hopes of economic stability.

Opposite: **This Buddha statue carved out of stone is located near the ancient Sri Lankan city of Anuradhapura.**

Anuradhapura and Polonnaruwa

Sri Lankan rulers built magnificent cities thousands of years ago. The ruins of many cities still stand today and are a reminder of Sri Lanka's ancient culture and history.

The most important of these cities is Anuradhapura, which was declared Sri Lanka's first capital city in 380 B.C. Anuradhapura remained the island's capital for more than a thousand years, and it is considered by Buddhists to be one of the most sacred places in Sri Lanka. The Indian emperor Aśoka sent his son with monks to Sri Lanka to spread Buddhism in the third century B.C. The emperor's daughter followed and brought a sapling of the sacred bo, or banyan, tree, from India, the type of tree under which Buddha attained enlightenment. She planted the sapling in Anuradhapura. The sacred bo tree is still found in Anuradhapura and is physically and spiritually central to the

Below: **The Abhayagiri dagoba is located in Anuradhapura.**

Left: These children are walking along the footpaths of a temple in Polonnaruwa. This city was the second capital of ancient Sri Lanka.

area. It is the oldest historically authenticated tree in the world and has been tended continuously for over two thousand years. Anuradhapura grew into a large and prosperous city. Many large structures were constructed, and at one time the city covered 20 square miles (52 square km). Today, visitors to Anuradhapura can see the remains of a large palace that used 1,600 columns to support a bronze roof.

Tamil kings from southern India periodically raided Sri Lanka for more than one thousand years, but the Sinhalese rulers kept control of Anuradhapura most of the time. Around the late tenth century, Anuradhapura was abandoned after it was occupied by invaders. A new capital was established in the eleventh century in Polonnaruwa, 65 miles (105 km) to the southeast. Over the next two hundred years, successive rulers added to the architectural expansion of the city. One notable project was the construction of a complex irrigation system of tanks and canals, which helped supply water to dry parts of the country. One of the most remarkable structures of that time was an irrigation embankment 36 feet (11 m) high and 10 miles (16 km) long that enclosed a 6,000-acre (2,428-hectare) irrigation lake. Polonnaruwa was eventually abandoned in the thirteenth century.

Above: A Buddhist dagoba towers over the trees in Polonnaruwa.

Beaches

Thousands of locals and foreigners relax and soak up the sun on Sri Lanka's beautiful beaches each year. Tourists from North America and Europe usually visit beaches in the southwestern part of Sri Lanka because the country's northern and eastern regions are affected by Sri Lanka's civil war. A small number of tourists, however, visit the white-sand beaches near Trincomalee on the east coast. Water sports are a favorite tourist activity. Water sports facilities near tourist resorts offer equipment, including jet skis, for rent. Snorkeling and scuba diving along coral reefs are also popular activities.

Above: **Sri Lanka is renowned for its beautiful beaches.**

Sri Lanka's southwestern, southern, and southeastern beaches, from Induruwa to Yala, are well-known nesting locations for sea turtles. Many people visit these areas to watch young turtles hatch.

The waters off Sri Lanka's coasts have a temperature of around 81° F (27° C) most of the year. Although the waters are usually calm, swimming can be dangerous during monsoon season. The sea is often choppy during this time, and the mixing of waters from the Indian Ocean, the Bay of Bengal, and the Arabian Sea produces strong currents that can drag swimmers underneath the water.

Many villages are located along Sri Lanka's coast. Besides enjoying the beaches, visitors can observe village craftsmen making dance masks and traders auctioning spices. Many of these villages are famous for their stilt fishermen, who perch atop poles to catch fish.

SCUBA FUN

Scuba divers can explore sunken ship wrecks in Sri Lanka's waters, although they have to be careful not to get trapped inside these vessels.

Stilt Fishing

Each stilt fisherman places a pole firmly into the seabed near shore. The fishermen then wade out to these poles and sit on the poles before casting their lines out to sea. The fishermen fish only when the sea and the fish are flowing in the right direction. The pole positions are passed on from father to son. The origins of this unique fishing method are unknown.

Above: **Fishermen on stilts wait patiently for fish to bite.**

Protecting the Beaches

Many of Sri Lanka's beaches are lined with coral reefs that contain unique animal and plant life. Unfortunately, some of these beaches have been damaged. Over the years, snorkelers and scuba divers have removed pieces of coral to keep as souvenirs. Visitors have also left garbage that has been washed out to sea, polluting the waters.

Recently, local groups have been trying to maintain the beauty and ecological balance of beaches by urging visitors to properly dispose of garbage. These groups also want to protect the coral reefs and are campaigning to keep hotels away from the waterfront.

Buddhist Dagobas

A dagoba is a shrine that contains relics related to the Buddha or his chief disciples. The relics kept in dagobas include teeth, bone fragments, or pieces from the sacred bo tree under which the Buddha reached enlightenment.

A dagoba resembles a dome with a spire on top. Elaborate carvings on the dagoba illustrate the story of Buddha's life. Ancient dagobas often had monasteries built nearby that could accommodate up to five thousand monks. Buddhist monks cut off ties with their families and lived simple lives of prayer and meditation.

One of Sri Lanka's largest dagobas, the Abhayagiri dagoba, was built in the ancient city of Anuradhapura around 100 B.C. The dagoba once measured about 330 feet (100 m) in height and rivaled the largest pyramids in Egypt. The Ruwanweli dagoba in Anuradhapura is considered one of the most sacred Buddhist sites in Sri Lanka. A wall carved with hundreds of elephants

Below: **The Ambasthale dagoba is among the most sacred places in Sri Lanka. This dagoba was built in the place where Mahinda, the son of the ancient Indian emperor Aśoka, converted the king of Sri Lanka to Buddhism.**

Above: **Statues of Buddha are often built near dagobas.**

protects the dagoba, which is popular among Sinhalese and overseas visitors. The Jetavanarama dagoba is believed to have once been over 330 feet (100 m) high, although after restoration it is now about 230 feet (70 m) high. Another important dagoba is the Mirisavati dagoba. According to legend, a Sri Lankan king named Dutugemunu plunged his spear — a symbol of royal authority — into the ground when he went to watch a water sports festival. Later, he could not pull the sword out of the ground. He regarded this as a divine message that the place was sacred, and he built the Mirisavati dagoba on this spot.

Guided by Astrology

Some historians believe that astrological beliefs guided the construction of the Mirisavati, Ruwanweli, and Jetavanarama dagobas. If the top points of the three dagobas are connected, they form a triangle that is perfectly aligned with a triangle of three stars on the right side of the Orion constellation. The Orion constellation has seven stars. Many Buddhists believe that three and seven are important numbers in the life of the Buddha.

JETAVANARAMA DAGOBA

The bricks used to make the Jetavanarama dagoba could be used to make a wall 10 feet (3 m) high and about 250 miles (400 km) long.

Civil War

Sri Lanka has been at war with Tamil rebels since 1983. The rebels are known as separatists because they want to create a separate homeland, known as Eelam, for Sri Lanka's Tamil people. The separatists believe they will no longer face discrimination from Sri Lanka's Sinhalese population if they are given their own land.

Since independence in 1948, the Sri Lankan government has introduced laws that discriminate against Tamils. In 1956, Sri Lankan prime minister S.W.R.D. Bandaranaike made Sinhalese the official language of the nation, even though nearly one-quarter of the population spoke Tamil. He also required the state to promote Buddhism and ignore other religions including Hinduism, Islam, and Christianity, which were practiced by millions of Sri Lankans. Bandaranaike's widow, Sirimavo, who succeeded him as prime minister, introduced laws that required Tamils to have higher grades than the Sinhalese to enter Sri Lankan universities and enforced her husband's language policy.

Below: **Troops from Sri Lanka's main Tamil separatist group, the Tamil Tigers, man a sandbag bunker in 1989.**

Left: Sri Lankan government forces survey the damage after a bomb explosion in 1989.

By the 1970s, several Tamil guerrilla groups had emerged. A flashpoint in tensions occurred in 1983 when a guerrilla group called the Tamil Tigers ambushed an army patrol and killed thirteen soldiers. As a result of this violent act, anti-Tamil riots broke out in many parts of Sri Lanka. Hundreds of thousands of Tamils then fled to the southern Indian state of Tamil Nadu, where people speak the same language and are culturally similar to Sri Lankan Tamils.

The Tamil Tigers gradually wiped out rival rebel groups and emerged as the main guerrilla force in Sri Lanka. Civil war still rages today and continues to take a terrible toll. Tens of thousands of Sri Lankans have been killed in the vicious cycle of fighting.

The Fighting Continues

Many countries are concerned about the continued violence that has prevented Sri Lanka's economy from growing. Norway has tried to arrange for government and rebel forces to negotiate a peaceful end to the fighting. Nevertheless, the Tamil Tigers and the Sri Lankan government have continued their military action. Sri Lankan Air Force planes still bomb guerrilla bases, while the Tamil Tigers continue their attacks on troops and civilians.

Below: Many Sri Lankans in Jaffna have built bomb shelters near their homes to protect their families.

Colombo

Colombo is Sri Lanka's capital. The city gained prominence about two hundred years ago when British rulers encouraged the establishment of commercial estates in nearby areas. After its harbor was built in the late 1800s, Colombo became the main commercial center of Sri Lanka.

More than one million people now live in Colombo. The city is open and green and boasts many parks, a long beach, and several lakes. The Galle Face Green, a grassy area extending for 1 mile (1.6 km) along Colombo's coast, comes alive in the mornings and evenings as children play cricket or soccer and adults exercise or walk along the beach. Galle Face Green also is a popular meeting place for young couples.

Colombo is divided into fifteen postal zones, and some people refer to areas of the city by postal code rather than by name. The central area, or Colombo 1, is called the Fort district because a fort was built there during the Portuguese and Dutch

KOTTE

Sri Jayewardenepura Kotte lies on the outskirts of Colombo. Formerly called Kotte, it was once the capital of a major Sinhalese kingdom. It is now the legislative capital of Sri Lanka.

Below: Colombo's Fort area houses many local and foreign businesses.

Above: **The Pettah district in Colombo has many shops that sell a wide variety of goods.**

eras. The area is now home to modern buildings. The Sri Lankan World Trade Center dominates the skyline. Two department stores, Cargills and Millers, are also located within the Fort district. These stores sell luxury goods, and their interiors feature wood paneling and brass fittings. Vendors on the sidewalks sell inexpensive clothes and knickknacks. Few trees line the streets in this area, and many people carry umbrellas to protect themselves from the hot sun.

The Pettah is a nearby business district where shops sell crafts, produce, and medicinal herbs. The streets are filled with pushcarts, trucks, motorcycles, bicycles, and people all trying to maneuver through the crowds. Bus conductors shout the destinations and routes that their buses will take. Three-wheel motor taxis are another popular form of transportation.

Colombo's main road, Galle Road, runs parallel with the coast and stretches from Colombo's city center south to the city of Galle. A long strip of hotels, offices, and houses line this road in Colombo.

Security in Colombo is tight. Roadblocks manned by personnel carrying automatic rifles are a common sight as Colombo has been a target of rebel bomb attacks.

Elephant Orphanage

The Pinnawela Elephant Orphanage is the first orphanage of its kind in the world. The orphanage, which was established in 1975, is home to about sixty elephants. Over the last thirty years, about half of Sri Lanka's forests have been cut down to make way for human settlements and plantations, leaving the country's wild elephants with little room to roam. Some of the elephants in the orphanage are babies that either wandered too far from the herd or were abandoned by their mothers when the herd separated. Other, older elephants were injured in the forests. Many of the orphanage's elephants were hurt by encounters with people.

Thousands of tourists visit Pinnawela each year to watch the elephants feed. The money earned through tourism helps pay for the elephants' food. The orphanage has also set up an elephant adoption scheme, through which donors are asked to provide powdered milk to help feed their "adopted" baby elephants.

Above: **Sri Lankan elephants live in the country's grasslands and forests. These elephants make their home in Pinnawela.**

A Day at the Orphanage

At the orphanage, elephant handlers feed the babies one gallon (3.8 liters) of milk five times a day in a small enclosure. At birth, baby elephants measure about 3 feet (0.9 m) tall and weigh about 200 pounds (91 kilograms). After feeding, the handlers usually let the elephants roam throughout the park. Adult elephants consume between 200 and 300 pounds (91 to 136 kg) of twigs, leaves, and grasses and between 50 and 60 gallons (189 l to 227 l) of water every day. Sometimes, they get a treat of sugarcane or unrefined sugar candy. Elephants have an inefficient digestive system and nearly half the food they eat is excreted as undigested matter. As a result, elephants spend most of their lives eating.

The elephants at Pinnawela are taken by their handlers to bathe twice a day in a nearby river. The handlers scrub the elephants down with coconut fiber. Elephants love water, and they sometimes swim away into deep water or refuse to come out of the stream. At the orphanage, adult elephants do light chores, such as hauling logs.

Saving the Asian Elephant

The Pinnawela orphanage is part of a worldwide effort to save the Asian elephant. The orphanage has an active breeding program, and many babies have been born there. Sri Lanka has approximately 2,500 to 3,000 elephants — 500 of which live in captivity. Sri Lankan elephants are slightly different from those found in other parts of Asia. Known as *Elephas maximus maximus*, the Sri Lankan elephant species is lighter in color than other elephant species, and few of the males have tusks. Without tusks, their chances of survival are higher because they are less likely to be killed by ivory poachers.

Above: **Visitors to Pinnawela watch as elephants bathe in a river located next to the Pinnawela elephant orphanage.**

Gems

Sri Lanka is sometimes called the "Pearl of the Indian Ocean" because it has the largest concentration of gems in the world. More than fifty types of gems, including sapphires, rubies, and amethysts, are found on the island.

The country's gem industry is one of the oldest in the world, and gems have been part of the country's history for fifteen centuries. Geological studies have revealed that about 20 percent of the land has gem deposits. In past centuries, European royalty often adorned themselves with jewelry studded with rare gems from Sri Lanka.

The major gem-producing area in Sri Lanka is centered around Ratnapura, which means "city of gems." It is a hilly region 65 miles (105 km) southeast of Colombo. Miners in this region look for a special layer of soil, known as *illama* (ILL-ah-mah), that is most likely to yield gemstones.

Above: **Many different types of gems, including sapphires and moonstones, can be found in Sri Lankan gem mines.**

Left: **A miner searches for gems in soil excavated from a Sri Lankan mine.**

Mining for Gems

After locating an illama, miners dig a vertical or horizontal mine shaft. The miners all work together. Some dig out the mineral deposits, others pump water from the tunnels, while a third group washes the muddy gravel. The owner of the land searches through the pebbles to find valuable stones. If a gemstone is found during the excavation, the profits are shared by all the workers.

Stones are cut by hand and later polished by hand or by machine. The value of a stone depends on its beauty, clarity, cut, and weight. Gems are weighed in carats.

Famous Gems

The blue sapphire is Sri Lanka's best-known gemstone and is among the most expensive and highly prized of all gems. A blue sapphire ranks second only to the diamond in hardness. The largest known sapphire, weighing 42 pounds (19 kg), was found in Sri Lanka. Another famous gem is the 182-carat Sri Lankan star sapphire that is displayed at the Smithsonian Museum of Natural History in Washington. Although found in Sri Lanka, this gem has been called the Star of Bombay.

Above: **This skilled craftsman is grinding gems that will be sold later. Gem grinding is a delicate process that takes years of practice to master.**

ILLEGAL MINES

In illegal mines, miners hire small children to go through narrow shafts to dig out gravel. This practice is banned by the government, but a few mines still ignore the law.

Hindu Temples

Hindus make up about 15 percent of Sri Lanka's population. Many Tamil areas, especially in the north and in cities such as Colombo, have colorful Hindu temples with elaborate sculptures. Also known as kovils, these temples are mostly built in honor of Shiva, one of the three main Hindu deities, who is worshiped as the God of Destruction. The two other main Hindu deities are Brahma, the God of Creation, and Vishnu, the God of Preservation. Hindus also worship hundreds of other minor deities.

Hindu temple architecture follows strict guidelines and pays close attention to small details. Sri Lankan temples resemble structures found in southern India. They are usually built with stone or brick and cement on sacred sites near groves, rivers, mountains, and springs. The entrances to most Hindu temples have tall gateways, known as gopurams, that have carvings of gods, goddesses, and their assistants. Several enclosures lead to a central hall, where idols of the main gods are located.

Below: **Elaborately decorated gateways, or gopurams, are a common feature of Hindu temples.**

Hindus take off their footwear before entering a temple. They then walk clockwise around the main shrine. During the prayers, a priest bathes, dresses, and decorates an idol with jewelry and flowers. Worshipers stand in an enclosure facing the idol and join in the chanting and singing. They offer fruits, flowers, and homemade sweets and burn camphor and incense sticks.

Above: **The statue in the middle of this picture represents Vishnu, the God of Preservation.**

Temple Restoration

Hundreds of Hindu temples were destroyed in the seventeenth century by Portuguese colonialists, who then used rubble from the temples to build walls to protect their forts. In the nineteenth century, a Sri Lankan spiritual leader named Arumuga Navalar (1822–1879) urged Hindus to rebuild the fallen temples, and many of them continue to do his work. One such example is the Koneswaran temple in Trincomalee. The temple was built about five thousand years ago but was destroyed in the seventeenth century. Restored in 1963, the temple is once again a grand structure with one thousand pillars and large amounts of gold and precious stones.

Masks

Masks are a popular part of Sri Lankan culture. One type of Sri Lankan mask is the kolam mask. Kolam masks cover only part of the wearer's face and are used in stage performances, which can have as many as forty characters. Traditionally, the performances dealt with pregnancy issues. The cravings of pregnant mothers were often believed to be caused by evil spirits, and the kolam dance was aimed at protecting the unborn baby. During British rule, many kolam performers also worked anti-colonial messages into their stage performances.

The *raksha* (RAHK-shah) is another type of mask that is worn by performers during festivals and processions. The most popular raksha masks show a demonic face with writhing cobras. Legend has it that Sri Lanka was once ruled by a race called the rakshas, or demons, who took on the form of cobras. People prayed to the *gurulu* (GOOH-rooh-looh), a mythical bird that eats snakes, for protection.

Below: **This masked statue is displayed at a street procession. Masks are believed to offer protection from evil spirits and illnesses.**

Masked Dances

In some parts of Sri Lanka, masked dances are performed to cure illnesses. Some Sri Lankans believe there are both natural and supernatural causes for diseases. When a disease cannot be cured by traditional methods, a ritual dance is sometimes performed.

The ceremony, which can last up to twelve hours, is held at night in an open arena. The patient sits on a low seat, while drummers tap a slow, rhythmic beat. A man wearing a mask slowly enters the arena, which is lit by flaming torches. At this point, the drums beat faster. The man spins around and shows his mask to the patient. The mask looks like a demon with bulging eyes, flared nostrils, and protruding teeth and is designed to inspire fear and awe. The dancer then leaps and spins in the air. During the frenzied dance, chants, and speeches, the shaman praises the demon's powers and tries to persuade the demon to leave. The dance is based on the belief that the demon must be appeased because it has the power to cause and cure diseases. While the ceremony is designed to cure the patient, it also provides an opportunity for spectators to openly discuss the troubles of the patient and the community.

Below: **This mask was made in Ambalangoda, a city famous for its complex mask carvings. Ambalangoda masks are highly prized by collectors.**

Perahera

The central town of Kandy comes alive with the sound of drums, cymbals, trumpets, fireworks, and dancers around July or August as elephants decorated in bright colors lead a procession known as Perahera. The dates of Perahera are decided by temple astrologers. People celebrate for ten nights, with the parades becoming increasingly extravagant each night. The parade in Kandy is the most famous one in Sri Lanka and is held in honor of the Temple of the Tooth, the most sacred shrine of the Sinhalese.

The parade originated hundreds of years ago as a victory celebration after war. The Sinhalese king, Magavanna, ordered the sacred tooth of the Buddha to be brought out of the temple in Kandy so that the public could pay their respects. In the last two hundred years, the ceremony has grown into a spectacle that attracts hundreds of thousands of people. The parade starts with a loud explosion. Hundreds of dancers leap and twirl in the air

Below: **The elephant procession is the highlight of Perahera. More elephants are added to the procession each night.**

as drummers beat out complicated tunes. Flame throwers, jugglers, students with colorful flags, men cracking long whips, and acrobats walk and dance in the parade. Dancers wearing special masks jump and scream as they try to ward off disease-causing demons.

Above: **These Buddhist monks are looking out over Perahera. The flag in the picture is a symbol of faith and peace used to represent Buddhism throughout the world.**

The excitement peaks late at night, when fifty or sixty elephants lumber through the main street of the town. The elephants are decorated in bright cloth, with blue, white, and pink light bulbs twinkling on their bodies. On the last night, processions start from the major shrines of Kandy, then eventually join. A column of decorated elephants follows each procession. The magnificent tusker elephant representing the Temple of the Tooth carries an illuminated wooden seat on its back. Temple attendants perched on the seat carry a replica of a casket containing the sacred tooth.

The parade ends with the ceremonial cleansing of a god's sword. The tooth relic is placed at the shrine. Four pots are filled with water from the center of the lake in Kandy and preserved until the following year. If the water in the pots evaporates before the year has ended, it is regarded as a sign of misfortune ahead.

Saris and Redde-hattes

Although Sri Lankan women wear many different styles of Western clothes, traditional clothing remains popular, especially in rural areas of the country. Many centuries ago, stitched clothes were not common. Frescoes in Sigiriya show women wearing a wraparound skirt and a loose piece of cloth to cover the upper body.

Saris

The sari is one type of traditional dress worn by Sri Lankan women. Saris are lengths of cloth 6 yards (5.5 m) long. Usually one end of the cloth is tucked into an underskirt; the cloth is then draped around the body, tucked, and pleated. The free end of the sari is draped loosely over the left shoulder or worn over the head as a hood. The sari is worn with a snug blouse.

There are many other ways to wear a sari. The Kandyan style, named after the city of Kandy, is very popular. For this style, the free end of the sari is worn over the right shoulder, instead of the

Below: **Saris are usually very colorful. White saris, however, are often worn by widows.**

left. Women usually wear Kandyan-style saris when they attend ceremonies. Some boutiques in Sri Lanka have recently begun selling two-piece dresses with long pleated skirts. Each dress has a folded strip of cloth worn over the shoulder. These garments are meant to look like saris.

Above: **Saris are made from many types of materials, from cotton to silk.**

Redde-hattes

Many Sri Lankan women prefer to wear the traditional *redde-hatte* (RED-e-HET-tuh) instead of a sari. The redde is a 7-foot (2-m) piece of cloth that is wrapped around the waist and falls to the ankles. The hatte is a small, tight blouse with a scooped-out neckline. Blouses may be sleeveless, or they may have puffed sleeves or sleeves that extend to the elbows. The modern version of a redde-hatte, worn by young girls, features a blouse with a frill around the neck. Women also usually wear their hair away from their faces while wearing the redde-hatte. They slick down their hair with coconut oil, part it in the middle, and tie it behind the neck in a bun. Jingling anklets, gold or silver bangles, and chunky necklaces complete the ensemble. The redde-hatte is worn especially during festivals, such as the Buddhist New Year.

Spices

For centuries, Sri Lankans have used spices to add flavor
and aroma to their food or to preserve pickles and chutneys.
Spices have also been used for medicinal purposes. Many of the
spices used around the world are grown in Sri Lanka. Although
inexpensive today, spices were once considered a luxury, even
by wealthy people. Since ancient times, the Romans, Greeks,
Portuguese, and Dutch have braved the rough seas to buy spices
from Sri Lanka. Spices are now one of Sri Lanka's major exports.

Spices are natural plant or vegetable products that are used
either whole or in powdered form to cook and preserve food.
Spices are taken from many parts of a plant, including flowers,
fruits, roots, and leaves.

Cinnamon, one of the main spices grown in Sri Lanka, comes
from a small, bushy tree belonging to the laurel family. The dried
inner bark is light brown and has a sweet flavor. Cinnamon is
often used in desserts, such as Sri Lankan Christmas cake. Sri

Below: **Spices such
as red chilis (*top,
left*) are important
ingredients in dishes
such as curries.**

Lankans also use cinnamon in vegetable and meat dishes such as curries. Cinnamon oil is rubbed onto a person's gums to relieve a toothache.

Other popular spices grown in Sri Lanka are cardamom, pepper, turmeric, and ginger. The fruit of the cardamom plant is handpicked, dried in the shade, and used as a seasoning in various dishes. Cardamom is sometimes added to tea. Sri Lankans also sometimes chew the fruit to freshen their breath.

Pepper is used raw to flavor pickles and salads or in a dried and powdered form in many Sri Lankan dishes. Sri Lankans drink pepper soup to clear a congested nose. Some Sri Lankans drink water in which a few peppercorns have been boiled to lose weight. Pepper can also be used as an insect repellent.

The dried roots of turmeric are ground into a bright yellow powder that is used to help digest food and as an antiseptic. Some Sri Lankans mix it in warm milk to relieve stomachaches.

The roots of the ginger plant are often used in vegetable and meat dishes to make them spicy. Sri Lankans eat candied ginger to aid digestion. Ginger is sometimes added to tea and soups to clear a congested nose.

FRUITS, ROOTS, AND MORE

Spices are taken from different parts of plants. These include fruits, such as coriander and chili peppers; parts of flowers, such as cloves and saffron; roots, such as turmeric and ginger; leaves, such as lemon grass and mint; kernels, such as nutmeg and coconuts; bark, such as cinnamon; and bulbs, such as garlic.

Tamil Tigers

Sri Lanka's main separatist group is called the Liberation Tigers of Tamil Eelam (LTTE). The LTTE is usually referred to as the Tamil Tigers or Tigers. Numbering between five thousand and fifteen thousand, the LTTE is one of the most feared guerrilla groups in the world. The LTTE has naval units, women's squads, and a suicide squad. LTTE supporters consider the suicide squad the most prestigious unit.

LTTE members follow a strict code of conduct. They do not drink alcohol or smoke, and most do not marry. The tiger is the symbol of the LTTE and represents the group's ferocity. The tiger symbol also contrasts with the lion, the symbol of the Sinhalese people, which is seen on Sri Lanka's national flag.

The LTTE emerged in the early 1970s, when a group of young people led by Velupillai Prabhakaran suggested that the Tamil-dominant areas of Sri Lanka gain independence from Sri Lanka. Although the idea was initially considered too radical, other Tamil political parties later supported the same view. The Sri Lankan government, however, feels the Tamil Tigers do not

Below: **LTTE recruits undergo rigorous training before being sent to combat. The LTTE has been criticized for recruiting teenagers below the age of seventeen.**

Above: **Female LTTE soldiers have fought just as fiercely as their male counterparts.**

represent Sri Lanka's entire Tamil population. Although many Tamils may agree with the government, most civilians are too frightened to criticize the LTTE in public. The Tamil Tigers run their own administration in the areas they control and impose taxes on the people living there. The LTTE also reportedly owns several ships registered in foreign countries and operates legitimate businesses under assumed names.

Human rights groups have accused the Tamil Tigers of using young children as shields while attacking the Sri Lankan military. Many children have reportedly been forced to quit school and join the LTTE. The LTTE denies these charges, asserting that the children who sign up with the group do so voluntarily.

The Tamil Tigers train in secret jungle camps. The guerrillas are promoted according to their performance in assigned missions and their devotion to the cause of Eelam, which is the formation of a Tamil homeland in northern and eastern Sri Lanka. LTTE fighters who are killed in battle are treated as heroes, and their names are painted on memorials in their villages.

Tea Estates

Tea is one of Sri Lanka's major exports. It is grown mostly in the southern and central hills of the country. The tea plant is rugged and adaptable and thrives in tropical climates. It will grow at any elevation from sea level to 8,000 feet (2,438 m) and in areas with an annual rainfall ranging between 50 and 300 inches (127 and 762 cm). Tea bushes also grow in many types of soil, including light sand, stiff clay, and even soil too poor for other crops.

Tea was brought to Sri Lanka from neighboring India in 1839 and first grown commercially by a Scot, James Taylor, in the 1860s. Most tea estates in Sri Lanka were first owned and managed by British companies. In 1971, the Sri Lankan government took over these estates. In recent years, the government has been encouraging private participation in managing the estates.

Above: **Tea accounts for about 25 percent of Sri Lanka's export earnings.**

Growing and Harvesting Tea

Thousands of varieties of tea exist in Sri Lanka because tea develops slightly different flavors and aromas depending on the soil in which it is grown, the climate, and the altitude. Leaves of

Below: **These workers are weighing tea leaves before sending them for processing at the tea factory.**

Above: **These workers are sifting tea leaves. This process helps group the leaves according to their size.**

plants grown at lower altitudes produce tea that has a rich color and strong body. Those growing at higher elevations are known for their aroma and flavor. Some companies buy Sri Lankan tea in bulk and blend it with teas from other countries to produce their own distinct flavors.

Sri Lanka's tea estates are located at altitudes of 3,000 to 8,000 feet (914 to 2,438 m). Although tea bushes can grow to a height of 30 feet (9 m), they are constantly pruned by workers. About 300,000 workers, most of them women, are involved in harvesting Sri Lanka's tea. As they glide through the bushes, they pluck the tea plant's top bud and its two youngest leaves and drop the bud and leaves into rattan baskets tied to their backs.

The plucked leaves are taken to factories, where they are slowly dried by blowers that circulate temperature-controlled air. Next, the leaves are crushed to begin the process of fermentation. Fermentation is a crucial period in the tea process as it determines the quality of the product. Afterward, the tea leaves are "fired," or dried at a high temperature, to seal in the flavor. No preservative or artificial flavoring is added. The tea is then sorted by color and particle size and packed for export to the Middle East, Europe, and North America.

TEA: A HEALTHY DRINK

Tea is believed to have medicinal properties if consumed in moderation. Drinking tea is believed to improve digestion and makes a person feel more energetic. Research also suggests that drinking tea improves immunity against cancer and heart disease. Drinking too much tea, however, can cause acidity and heartburn.

Women Leaders

When Sirimavo Ratwatte Dias Bandaranaike was elected prime minister of Sri Lanka in 1960, she became the first woman prime minister in the world. Usually known as "Mrs. B.," she held the post of prime minister three times: from 1960 to 1965, 1970 to 1977, and 1994 to 2000.

Mrs. Bandaranaike was born in Sri Lanka in 1916. In 1940, she married S.W.R.D. Bandaranaike, who was Sri Lanka's prime minister from 1956 to 1959. After her husband's assassination in 1959, Sirimavo Bandaranaike assumed the leadership of the Sri Lanka Freedom Party (SLFP). When the SLFP won the national elections in 1960, Mrs. Bandaranaike became prime minister. She changed the name of the country from Ceylon to Sri Lanka in 1972.

Mrs. B died on October 10, 2000, at the age of 84. Although some of her policies, such as changing Sri Lanka's official language from English to Sinhala, were controversial, Mrs. Bandaranaike earned respect for being a strong and charismatic leader. She was also a prominent leader of the Non-Aligned Movement, a political grouping of countries that did not ally themselves with the United States or the Soviet Union during the Cold War.

Left: **Sirimavo Bandaranaike (*right*) made history when she became the first woman prime minister in the world.**

Left: **Chandrika Kumaratunga (***behind podium***) regained her family's dominance of Sri Lankan politics when she was elected president in 1994.**

Following in Mother's Footsteps

In 1994, Chandrika Bandaranaike Kumaratunga, Sirimavo Banadaranaike's daughter, became president of Sri Lanka. She then appointed her mother as prime minister. Born in Colombo in 1945, Kumaratunga has a degree in political science from the University of Paris.

After being elected as Sri Lanka's president, Kumaratunga immediately began to change her mother's policies. She steered Sri Lanka towards a free market economy and has made efforts to end Sri Lanka's civil war. Kumaratunga began talks with Tamil Tiger guerrillas, but when negotiations failed, she stepped up military attacks against the separatists. In 2001 parliamentary elections, Kumaratunga's political party, the People's Alliance (PA), suffered a setback when it was defeated by Ranil Wickremesinghe's United National Party (UNP). The UNP and its allies won 114 of the 225 seats in Sri Lanka's parliament. Wickremesinghe is now Sri Lanka's prime minister. Kumaratunga remains Sri Lanka's president until the country's next presidential elections in 2005.

RELATIONS WITH NORTH AMERICA

Sri Lanka enjoys a warm relationship with the United States and Canada, based partly on the countries' shared democratic and economic traditions. Economic relations between the United States and Sri Lanka stretch back as far as the eighteenth century, when a ship from the United States sailed into Galle, a Sri Lankan port. The United States also played an important role in the revival of Buddhism in Sri Lanka in the late nineteenth century. About a quarter of a million Sri Lankans live in North America, and thousands of tourists from the United States and Canada visit Sri Lanka every year. Other North Americans in Sri Lanka

Below: **These hats in a Sri Lankan street stall feature logos of a number of Sri Lankan and U.S. movies.**

include aid workers, journalists, researchers, and diplomats. The United States is the largest importer of Sri Lankan goods. Most Sri Lankans learn much about the United States and Canada from books and magazines, as well as from Hollywood movies and rock music.

Although the United States and Canada did not pay much attention to Sri Lankan affairs in the past, Sri Lanka's ongoing civil war has attracted global attention. The United States and Canada are just two of the many countries around the world that hope for a peaceful end to the fighting.

Opposite: **Sri Lankans gather to attend a service at a Roman Catholic church in the city of Negombo. Missionaries from the United States helped spread Christianity among Sri Lanka's population.**

Left: **This illustration depicts the port of Galle, which the first U.S. ship sailed into in 1789.**

Early Relations

Christian missionaries, who came to convert Buddhists and Hindus to Christianity, were among the first North Americans to come to Sri Lanka.

Trade relations between the United States and Sri Lanka date back to the eighteenth century, when the first ship sailed from the United States into the southern port of Galle in 1789. Ice from New England ponds was traded for Sri Lankan graphite, later used to make pencils for children in the United States.

In 1850, American John Black was appointed commercial officer in Galle. His main responsibility was to improve trade between the United States and Ceylon, as the country was then known. Black's letter to the State Department on December 16, 1850, was the first official dispatch from Sri Lanka to the United States. A U.S. consulate was established in 1875. As a sign of the improving commercial ties between the two countries, the Singer Company of the United States opened an office selling sewing machines in Colombo in 1877. This event marked the first direct investment in Sri Lanka by a company from the United States.

Olcott and the Buddhist Revival

In the 1870s, American Henry Steele Olcott backed Sri Lankans by organizing a campaign to revive Buddhism in Sri Lanka. Olcott founded the Theosophical Society of Ceylon, which established three colleges: Ananda College, Mahinda College, and Dharmaraja College. The society also established hundreds of schools to teach students about Buddhism. In addition, the society persuaded the British governor of Sri Lanka to make Vesak, Buddhism's biggest festival, a public holiday. Olcott designed the six-colored Buddhist flag that is used to represent Buddhism throughout the world

World War II and Independence

During World War II, U.S. troops were stationed in Sri Lanka to help fight against the Japanese. Canadian Air Force personnel were also stationed in Sri Lanka during this period. After the war, in 1948, Sri Lanka gained its independence from the British, and the United States set up an embassy in Colombo shortly after. Canada later established a High Commission in Colombo, Sri Lanka's capital city.

Above: **Henry Steele Olcott helped revive the Buddhist faith in Sri Lanka.**

Below: **Buddhism is now the most popular religion in Sri Lanka, thanks partly to the efforts of American Henry Steele Olcott.**

Post-Independence

After gaining independence, Sri Lanka maintained good relations with both the Soviet Union and the United States. In 1958, the United States signed an agreement to provide Sri Lanka with technical assistance and money for economic projects. In the 1960s, Sri Lanka became one of the first countries to join the Non-Aligned Movement, a group of countries that did not wish to ally themselves to either the United States or the Soviet Union.

Strained Relations

When Sri Lanka's prime minister Sirimavo Bandaranaike faced a violent communist revolt in 1971, the United States and Canada helped crush the uprising. In the mid-1970s, relations between Sri Lanka and the United States became strained, however, when the Sri Lankan government took control of many private companies in Sri Lanka, including U.S. companies such as Caltex and Shell. This move angered the U.S. government, which responded by cutting off all financial aid to Sri Lanka, adding to Sri Lanka's economic problems. Relations between the two countries reached a low point.

Below: **Although relations between the United States and Sri Lanka have improved greatly since the 1970s, the two countries still experience occasional friction. This picture shows Sri Lankans staging a protest outside the U.S. embassy in Sri Lanka. The protestors feel the United States and other industrialized countries are not doing enough to help Sri Lanka's economy.**

Rebuilding Ties

In 1977, a new government led by President Junius Richard Jayewardene swept into power in Sri Lanka. Jayewardene's government immediately began to seek closer relations with the United States and Canada. Since then, economic relations between the three countries have gradually improved. The United States is now the largest importer of Sri Lankan goods.

The United States has also made several trade agreements with Sri Lanka, including an Open-Skies aviation agreement that was signed in 2001. This agreement will eventually remove all restrictions on passenger flights between Sri Lanka and the United States.

In 2000, Ashley Wills, the U.S. ambassador to Sri Lanka, and Lakshman Kadirgamar, Sri Lanka's minister of foreign affairs, unveiled a plaque at the U.S. Embassy in Sri Lanka. The commemorative plaque marks the 150th anniversary of established relations between the two countries. Sri Lanka also issued a new postage stamp in 2001 to celebrate this anniversary.

Above: During his visit to the United States in 1984, Sri Lankan president Junius Richard Jayewardene presented U.S. president Ronald Reagan (*second from right*) with a baby elephant as a gift.

Immigration

Many Sri Lankans have settled in North America in recent years. Thousands of Sri Lankans now live in the United States — mostly in large cities such as New York, Chicago, Houston, Los Angeles, and San Francisco. In 2000, nearly 3,000 Sri Lankans emigrated to Canada. Some of these emigrants arrived in Canada as refugees after their homes were destroyed and their family members killed during Sri Lanka's civil war. Other Sri Lankans came to Canada seeking political asylum, claiming LTTE guerrillas or the military would kill them if they went back to Sri Lanka. Many Sri Lankan children who lost both their parents during the war have been adopted by American and Canadian families. Upon arriving in North America, many Sri Lankan immigrants continue to nurture and foster their ethnic and religious identities.

Some Sri Lankan immigrants in North America own small businesses or work in supermarkets and restaurants. Others study at universities, conduct research in science laboratories, work as doctors and nurses, or pursue other professions. A number of Sri Lankan scientists, such as Ray Jayawardhana, are famous in their fields. In 1998, Jayawardhana, a 27-year-old Sri Lankan astronomer, led a team of scientists that discovered another solar system forming around a distant star. Jayawardhana, who was studying for his doctorate at Harvard University, found a ring of dust around the star HR 4796. This ring is several times brighter and larger than the Sun. In 2001, Jayawardhana won a three-year Miller's Fellowship to attend the University of California, Berkeley.

Sri Lankan-born Michael Ondaatje is one of the world's most famous novelists. Raised in London, Ondaatje later became a Canadian citizen and taught for many years at York University in Toronto. Ondaatje won the 1992 Booker Prize for his novel *The English Patient*, which was later made into an Academy Award-winning movie.

Sri Lanka's fastest sprinter, Susanthika Jayasinghe, lives in Los Angeles and trains under U.S. coach Tony Campbell. In the women's 200-meter race at the Olympic Games in 2000, she won a bronze medal, setting her best time of 22.28 seconds.

JAYAWARDHANA'S INSPIRATION

Ray Jayawardhana's interest in science was sparked when he met Dr. Cyril Ponnamperuma, a famous Sri Lankan scientist living in the United States. Ponnamperuma was best known for his work in the field of chemical evolution and the origin of life. From 1984 until his death in 1994, Ponnamperuma acted as the science and technology adviser to the Sri Lankan president.

Left: Susanthika Jayasinghe holds up the Sri Lankan flag after winning a bronze medal in the 2000 Olympic Games in Sydney, Australia. Jayasinghe is the first woman Sri Lankan to win an Olympic medal. She is also the first Sri Lankan to win an Olympic medal in over fifty years.

North Americans in Sri Lanka

Both the United States and Canada have embassies in Sri Lanka to look after their interests in the country. Despite Sri Lanka's civil war, many U.S. citizens and Canadians live in Sri Lanka. They work with aid organizations such as the International Committee of the Red Cross, the Canadian International Development Agency (CIDA), and the United States Agency for International Development (USAID).

Aid Workers

Aid workers play an important role in Sri Lanka. They are often the only source of medical help to people trapped in the war zone. Aid workers act as mediators between the guerrillas and the government and help organize the exchange of the bodies of those killed in the fighting.

Left: **A member of the Canadian Air Force (*right*) places a Canadian flag near a gravestone in a Sri Lankan cemetery as part of a Remembrance Day ceremony that honors soldiers who have fought and died for their countries.**

Above: **A Sri Lankan soldier armed with a U.S. rifle patrols the streets of Sri Lanka.**

Peace Corps volunteers were once active in Sri Lanka. These volunteers taught English and crafts to children, assisted nurses and doctors in hospitals, and trained villagers in preventative healthcare, hygiene, and other useful skills. Due to concerns over the safety of its volunteers during the country's civil war, the Peace Corps removed its volunteers from the country in 1998.

USAID helps the Sri Lankan government and private companies compete with other countries in key industries, such as tea, rubber, tourism, jewelry, and information technology. The U.S. government also helps Sri Lanka fight drug abuse among its people by giving funds to support volunteer groups.

Academic Ties

Since 1952, the United States and Sri Lanka have had an academic exchange program as part of the Fulbright program. Many interns from North American universities conduct research in Sri Lankan research institutes. These students and scholars in Sri Lanka research topics that include conflict, multiculturalism, and development.

MILITARY AID

Military officers from the United States train Sri Lankan armed forces in first aid, reconnaissance techniques, and aircraft maintenance. Many Sri Lankan officers attend military courses in military academies in the United States.

Above: **A poster for Pepsi hangs in this street stall in Sri Lanka. Pepsi is just one of many North American businesses operating in Sri Lanka.**

North American Businesses

Many businesspeople from North America live in Sri Lanka, since major banks and insurance companies have offices in Colombo. Symbols of U.S. businesses, including Coca-Cola, Federal Express, and Pizza Hut, can be seen in many parts of Sri Lanka. About fifty companies from the United States operate in Sri Lanka, and approximately 350,000 men and women working in eight hundred factories in Sri Lanka produce clothes for North American retailers, such as Nike and Columbia Sportswear. Over 60 percent of garments exported by Sri Lanka go to the United States. The United States bought almost U.S. $2 billion worth of Sri Lankan items in 2000, including clothes, tea, and gems. At the same time, Sri Lanka imported about U.S. $255 million worth of American wheat, electronics, and consumer goods.

Wheat

Sri Lankans love bread even though no wheat can be grown on the tropical island. Nearly half the wheat sold in Sri Lanka comes from the United States. In times of need, the United States has donated wheat to Sri Lanka. Since 1950, the United States has provided Sri Lanka with about U.S. $1 billion in wheat. In 2001, the United States signed an agreement to provide Sri Lanka with about U.S. $8 million of wheat. The wheat provided under this agreement helps relieve poverty-stricken areas of Sri Lanka and forms about 7 percent of the total amount of wheat eaten in Sri Lanka annually.

United against Terrorism

The United States and Sri Lanka share a common stand on terrorism. The U.S. State Department has listed the LTTE, a guerrilla group that is fighting for a separate Tamil state in Sri Lanka, as a foreign terrorist organization and has banned it from raising funds in the United States. Following the terrorist attacks on the United States on September 11, 2001, the United States expressed its continued support of the Sri Lankan government's policy regarding the LTTE. While the United States believes Sri Lanka has a right to defend itself against acts of terrorism, the U.S. government has also urged Sri Lanka to seek a peaceful solution to the civil war.

Below: **These Sri Lankan factory workers are busy sewing stuffed toys that will be exported to the United States.**

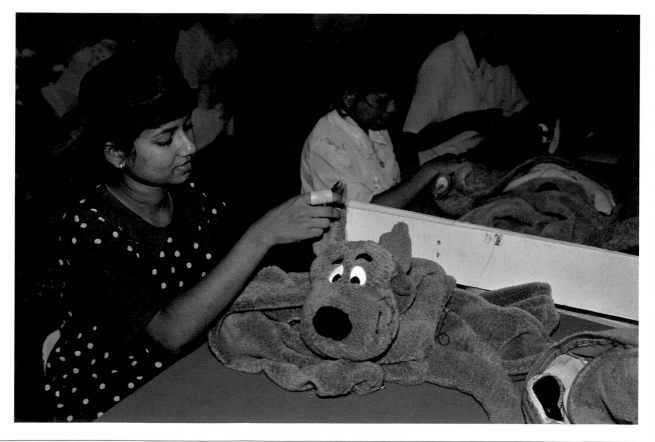

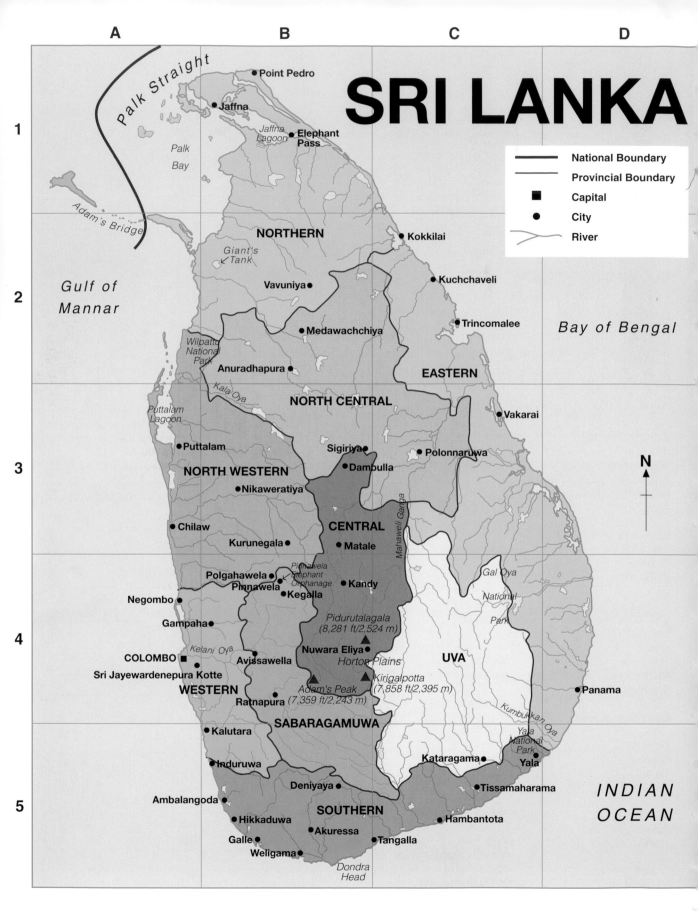

SRI LANKA

Above: These fishermen are unloading their catch at a small coastal harbor in Sri Lanka.

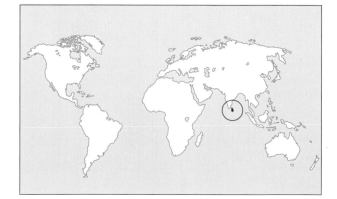

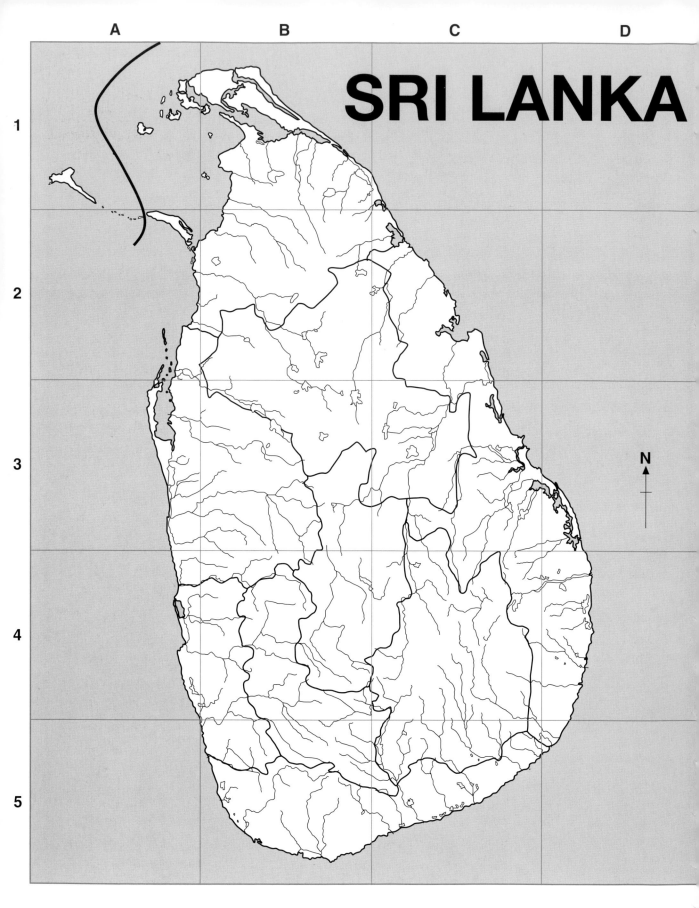

SRI LANKA

Above: **This young farmer in the central region of Sri Lanka is hard at work harvesting his crops.**

How Is Your Geography?

Learning to identify the main geographical areas and points of a country can be challenging. Although it may seem difficult at first to memorize the locations and spellings of major cities or the names of mountain ranges, rivers, deserts, lakes, and other prominent physical features, the end result of this effort can be very rewarding. Places you previously did not know existed will suddenly come to life when referred to in world news, whether in newspapers, television reports, other books and reference sources, or on the Internet. This knowledge will make you feel a bit closer to the rest of the world, with its fascinating variety of cultures and physical geography.

Used in a classroom setting, the instructor can make duplicates of this map using a copy machine. (PLEASE DO NOT WRITE IN THIS BOOK!) Students can then fill in any requested information on their individual map copies. Used one-on-one, the student can also make copies of the map on a copy machine and use them as a study tool. The student can practice identifying place names and geographical features on his or her own.

Sri Lanka at a Glance

Official Name Democratic Socialist Republic of Sri Lanka

Capital Colombo (Sri Jayewardenepura Kotte is the legislative capital.)

Languages Sinhala (official and national), Tamil (national)

Population 19.4 million

Land Area 25,332 square miles (65,610 square km)

Provinces Central, Eastern, North Central, North Western, Northern, Sabaragamuwa, Southern, Uva, Western

Highest Point Pidurutalagala 8,281 feet (2,524 m)

Major Mountains Adam's Peak, Kirigalpotta

Longest River Mahaweli Ganga

Main Religions Buddhism, Hinduism, Islam, Christianity

Important Leaders Solomon Bandaranaike (1899–1959)

Sirimavo Bandaranaike (1916–2000)

Chandrika Kumaratunga (1945–)

Ranil Wickremesinghe (1949–)

Major Festivals and Holidays Sinhalese and Tamil New Year (April 14)

Vesak (May)

Deepavali (October/November)

Christmas (December 25)

Perahera (July/August)

Currency Sri Lankan rupee (LKR 92.8 = U.S. $1 as of 2002)

Opposite: **Buddhist statues and temples are located in many parts of Sri Lanka.**

Glossary

Sinhala Vocabulary

aluva (AH-loo-ah): a rice-flour fudge.

Ayubovan (AH-yooh-boh-vahn): welcome.

baila (BY-lah): an energetic and pulsating musical style.

dagobas (DAH-go-bahs): Buddhist shrines.

gurulu (GOOH-rooh-looh): a mythical bird that eats snakes.

hoppers (hop-PERS): a rice-based dish.

illama (ILL-ah-mah): a layer of soil that often contains gemstones.

kotta pora (koh-TAH POH-rah): a Sri Lankan game that involves pillow fighting.

olinda kaliya (oh-LIN-dah KAH-lee-yah): a board game played with seeds.

Perahera (peh-RAH-HEH-rah): a Buddhist procession held in July or August.

pittu (pit-TOOH): rice flour and grated coconut steamed in a bamboo tube.

raksha (RAHK-shah): a mask worn during festivals and processions.

redde-hatte (RED-e-HET-tuh): a traditional type of clothing commonly worn by Sri Lankan women.

rotty (ROH-tea): a soft tortilla with meat and vegetables or onions and chili peppers.

sambal (SAHM-bahl): coconut and chili peppers ground together and eaten as a spicy side dish.

sri (SHREE): auspicious; promising success.

vadai (VAH-day): a deep-fried patty made of lentils and flour.

Veddahs (VED-duhs): indigenous inhabitants of Sri Lanka.

wattalappam (WAH-TAHL-ah-pum): an egg pudding with a caramel-like flavor.

Tamil Vocabulary

Brahman (BRAH-mahn): an all-encompassing force that is the core belief of Hindus.

Eelam (EE-lahm): precious land; the name Tamil separatists give to the homeland they wish to create in Sri Lanka.

gopurams (go-POOH-rahms): tall, brightly colored gateways that lead to Hindu temples.

kaasu (KAH-sooh): ready money.

kolam (KOH-lahm): costume; dramatic dance.

kovils (KOH-vills): Hindu temples.

Thai Pongal (THIGH POHNG-gahl): a Hindu harvest festival.

Thaipusam (THIGH-POO-sum): Hindu festival of human endurance and self-sacrifice.

Vanakkam (vah-nah-KAHM): welcome.

Arabic Vocabulary

Id-ul-Fitr (eed-OOL-FIT-ruh): a festival celebrating the end of Ramadan.

Milad-un-Nabi (MEE-LAHD-un-nah-bee): a Muslim festival celebrating the birth of the Prophet Mohammed.

Malay Vocabulary

ketayap (kur-TAH-yahp): a headdress worn by Muslim men and boys.

English Vocabulary

alliance: an association to further the common interests of its members.

antiseptic: a substance that kills germs and harmful bacteria.

appeased: pacified; brought to a state of calm.

astrologer: a person who studies the movement and interaction of stars and planets to predict future events.

auspicious: promising success; favorable.

bo tree: also known as the banyan tree. Buddha sat under this tree when he attained enlightenment.

Burghers: descendents of Portuguese-Sinhalese and Dutch-Sinhalese peoples.

chutney: a relish or sauce of Indian origin, made of fruit, vinegar, sugar, and spices.

dharma: the Buddhist and Hindu belief in correct action and conforming to duty.

deities: gods or goddesses.

dowry: money and goods a wife brings to her husband at marriage.

excreted: separated and expelled from the blood or tissues as waste.

exorcise: seek to expel an evil spirit by religious or solemn ceremonies.

flashpoint: the stage or point at which an event or situation becomes critical.

frescoes: pictures painted on plastered walls when the plaster is wet.

guerrilla: a soldier who forms an unofficial army to fight against an existing political order.

herald: signal the coming of; usher in.

indigenous: originating in or characteristic of a particular region or country.

judiciary: a system of courts of law.

lagoons: areas of shallow water separated from the ocean by low sandy dunes.

monsoon: the season in southern and Southeast Asia characterized by long periods of heavy rainfall.

negotiate: to settle differences between two or more groups of people through nonviolent means, such as conferences, discussions, and compromise.

palm leaves: strips of treated leaves on which scriptures were etched with a metal pin.

penance: a punishment that makes up for a wrongdoing or sin.

poachers: people who trespass on private property or catch fish or hunt game illegally.

province: an administrative district or division of a country.

pyre: a pile of wood or other flammable material used for burning a dead body.

relinquished: gave up; renounced.

Sanskrit: an ancient Indian language from which Pali and Sinhala originated.

sari: a traditional wraparound garment worn by women in Sri Lanka and India.

separatists: people who support the independence or autonomy of a certain area in a larger political unit.

shaman: a person who acts as an intermediary between the natural and supernatural worlds, using magic to cure illness, foretell the future, and control spiritual forces.

snorkeling: swimming submerged with only a tube, known as a snorkel, above the surface of the water to supply air.

subsidized: aided or promoted with public money.

terrorist: a person who commits acts of violence, usually against civilians, to draw attention to his or her cause.

traits: distinguishing qualities of a person's appearance or character.

More Books to Read

Aliya: Stories of the Elephants of Sri Lanka. Teresa Cannon and Peter David (Airavata Press)

Buddhism. Religions of Mankind series. Julien Ries (Chelsea House)

Divali. A World of Holidays series. Dilip Kadodwala (Raintree/Steck-Vaughn)

A Field Guide to the Birds of Sri Lanka. John Harrison (Oxford University Press)

The Food of Sri Lanka: Authentic Recipes from the Island of Gems. Douglas Bullis and Wendy Hutton (Tuttle Publishing)

Hinduism. World Beliefs and Cultures series. Sue Penney (Heinemann)

Sri Lanka. Robert Zimmermann (Children's Press)

Sri Lanka. Cultures of the World series. Nanda Pethiyagoda Wanasundera (Benchmark Books)

Sri Lanka in Pictures. Visual Geography series. (Lerner)

Sri Lanka: War-Torn Island. World in Conflict series. Lawrence J. Zwier (Lerner)

Videos

Elephant. National Geographic Video Classics series. (National Geographic)

Just the Facts: Families in the Wild — Monkeys. (Goldhil)

Web Sites

lcweb2.loc.gov/frd/cs/lktoc.html

withanage.tripod.com/index.html

www.lankalibrary.com

www.lanka.net/ctb/index.html

www.srilankaembassyusa.org

Due to the dynamic nature of the Internet, some web sites stay current longer than others. To find additional web sites, use a reliable search engine with one or more of the following keywords to help you locate information about Sri Lanka. Keywords: *Sirimavo Bandaranaike, Buddhism, Ceylon, Colombo, elephant orphanage, Sinhalese, Tamils.*

Index